Python Programming For Workflow Automation

A Comprehensive Guide To Automating Tasks, Processes And Systems With Python Scripting

Bronson E. Lee

Table Of Content

DISCLAIMER

The authors and publishers of "Python Programming For Workflow Automation" have diligently striven to ensure the accuracy and completeness of the information contained within this book at the time of publication. However, it is crucial to acknowledge that the field of software development, including Workflow Automation, is characterized by rapid advancements and evolving best practices.

Therefore, the authors and publishers offer no warranty, express or implied, regarding the enduring accuracy, completeness, suitability, or effectiveness of the information presented herein. Readers are strongly encouraged to remain abreast of the latest developments in Workflow Automation, associated technologies, and industry best practices through continued learning and engagement with relevant resources.

The authors and publishers shall not be held liable for any errors, omissions, or any losses or damages of any kind arising from the use of, or reliance upon, the information contained within this book. This includes, but is not limited to, incidental, consequential, or punitive damages.

The code examples provided in this book are intended for illustrative purposes only and may necessitate modification to suit specific applications or environments. The reader assumes full responsibility for the implementation and consequences of utilizing any code, techniques, or methodologies described herein.

All trademarks, trade names, and logos mentioned in this book are the property of their respective owners. Any references to third-party resources, websites, or materials are provided for convenience and informational purposes only. The authors and publishers do not endorse or assume any responsibility for the content, accuracy, or availability of such external resources.

By utilizing the information presented in this book, the reader acknowledges and agrees to the terms of this disclaimer.

INTRODUCTION

In today's technology-driven world, efficiency reigns supreme. The ability to automate tasks, streamline processes, and optimize workflows is no longer a luxury, but a necessity. This book, **Python Programming for Workflow Automation**, serves as your comprehensive guide to harnessing the power of Python to achieve unprecedented levels of productivity and effectiveness.

Whether you're a seasoned professional seeking to eliminate tedious manual tasks or a curious beginner eager to explore the world of automation, this book will equip you with the knowledge and skills to transform the way you work. We'll embark on a journey that starts with the fundamentals of Python programming and culminates in the creation of sophisticated automation solutions.

Why Python for Automation?

Python, renowned for its readability and versatility, has emerged as the language of choice for automation. Its extensive libraries and frameworks provide a rich toolkit for tackling a wide range of automation challenges. From interacting with the operating system and web services to manipulating data and controlling applications, Python offers the flexibility and power to automate virtually any task.

What You'll Learn

This book is carefully structured to guide you through the essential concepts and techniques of Python automation. We'll start with the basics, laying a solid foundation in Python programming. You'll learn about data types, variables, control flow, and functions, the building blocks of any Python script.

Then, we'll delve into the practical applications of Python automation. You'll discover how to:

- **Automate web tasks:** Scrape data from websites, interact with APIs, and control web browsers.
- **Streamline system administration:** Manage files and directories, schedule tasks, and interact with the operating system.
- **Enhance communication:** Send and receive emails, and integrate with messaging platforms like Slack.
- **Control graphical applications:** Automate interactions with desktop applications using GUI automation techniques.

- **Harness the power of databases:** Connect to databases, extract and manipulate data, and generate reports.
- **Build robust and reliable automation:** Implement error handling, debugging techniques, and testing strategies.
- **Unlock the potential of machine learning:** Introduce basic machine learning concepts and apply them to create intelligent automation solutions.

Throughout the book, you'll find clear explanations, practical examples, and hands-on exercises that reinforce your learning and help you apply the concepts to real-world scenarios. We'll also explore advanced techniques and best practices to ensure your automation solutions are efficient, maintainable, and scalable.

Who Should Read This Book

This book is designed for a wide audience, including:

- **System administrators:** Seeking to automate repetitive tasks and improve system efficiency.
- **Data analysts:** Wanting to automate data extraction, processing, and reporting.

- **Web developers:** Interested in automating web scraping, testing, and interactions with web services.
- **Business professionals:** Aiming to automate workflows and improve productivity.
- **Students and enthusiasts:** Eager to learn Python programming and its applications in automation.

Embark on Your Automation Journey

Whether you're a novice or an experienced programmer, this book will empower you to embrace the world of automation. With Python as your tool and this book as your guide, you'll be well-equipped to automate tasks, streamline processes, and unlock new levels of efficiency in your work and personal life.

So, let's begin this exciting journey into the world of Python automation!

Part I: Foundations of Python for Workflow Automation

Chapter 1: Introduction to Workflow Automation with Python

What is Workflow Automation?

In today's fast-paced digital world, efficiency is paramount. Businesses and individuals alike are constantly seeking ways to streamline their operations, reduce manual effort, and optimize productivity. This is where workflow automation comes into play.

Workflow automation is the process of using software to automate repetitive, rule-based tasks and processes. It involves designing and implementing systems that can automatically execute a sequence of actions, often without the need for human intervention. By automating these tasks, we can free up valuable time and resources, allowing us to focus on more strategic and creative endeavors.

Imagine a scenario where a company receives hundreds of emails daily. Manually sorting, categorizing, and responding to each email would be a tedious and time-consuming task. However, with workflow automation, this process can be streamlined. An automated system can be set up to filter emails based on specific criteria, forward them to the appropriate departments, and even generate automated responses for common inquiries.

This is just one example of how workflow automation can transform the way we work. From simple tasks like sending automated email reminders to complex processes like onboarding new employees, the possibilities are endless.

The Benefits of Workflow Automation

Workflow automation offers a multitude of benefits, including:

- **Increased Efficiency:** By automating repetitive tasks, we can significantly reduce the time and effort required to complete them. This leads to faster turnaround times and improved overall efficiency.
- **Reduced Errors:** Human error is inevitable, especially when performing repetitive tasks. Automation eliminates the risk of manual errors, ensuring greater accuracy and consistency.
- **Improved Productivity:** By freeing up employees from mundane tasks, automation allows them to focus on more challenging and rewarding work. This can lead to

increased job satisfaction and higher productivity levels.

- **Enhanced Collaboration:** Automation can facilitate seamless collaboration between different teams and departments by automating the flow of information and tasks.
- **Cost Savings:** By optimizing processes and reducing manual effort, automation can lead to significant cost savings in the long run.
- **Better Compliance:** Automated systems can be designed to ensure adherence to regulatory requirements and internal policies, minimizing the risk of compliance breaches.

Key Components of a Workflow

To effectively automate a workflow, it's essential to understand its key components:

- **Input:** This refers to the initial trigger or data that initiates the workflow. It could be an incoming email, a form submission, or a scheduled event.
- **Steps:** These are the individual actions or tasks that need to be performed within the workflow. Each step has a specific purpose and contributes to the overall goal of the workflow.

- **Conditions:** These are rules or criteria that determine the flow of the workflow. Based on certain conditions, the workflow may branch out into different paths or trigger specific actions.
- **Outputs:** This is the final outcome or result of the workflow. It could be a generated report, a notification sent to a user, or an updated record in a database.

By carefully defining these components, we can create well-structured and efficient workflows that can be easily automated.

Workflow Automation in Different Industries

Workflow automation has applications across a wide range of industries. Here are a few examples:

- **Customer Service:** Automating tasks like ticket routing, response generation, and customer follow-up can significantly improve customer satisfaction and response times.
- **Human Resources:** Automating processes like onboarding, performance reviews, and payroll management can streamline HR operations and enhance employee experience.

- **Marketing:** Automating email campaigns, social media posting, and lead nurturing can help marketers reach a wider audience and generate more leads.
- **Finance:** Automating tasks like invoice processing, expense approvals, and financial reporting can improve accuracy and efficiency in financial operations.

The Role of Python in Workflow Automation

Python, with its versatility, extensive libraries, and ease of use, has emerged as a powerful tool for workflow automation. Its ability to interact with various systems, manipulate data, and automate tasks makes it an ideal choice for building robust and efficient automation solutions. In the following chapters, we will explore the various Python libraries and techniques that can be used to automate a wide range of workflows.

Why Python for Automation?

While numerous programming languages can be employed for automation, Python has emerged as a dominant force and preferred choice in the field. This popularity is not merely a coincidence; Python possesses a unique combination of features that make it exceptionally well-suited for automation tasks.

1. Simplicity and Readability

Python's syntax is renowned for its clarity and resemblance to natural language. This readability makes it easier to learn, write, and maintain automation scripts. Even those with limited programming experience can quickly grasp the fundamentals and begin automating tasks with Python. This ease of use is crucial in automation, where the focus should be on solving problems rather than grappling with complex syntax.

2. Extensive Libraries and Frameworks

Python boasts a vast ecosystem of libraries and frameworks specifically designed for automation. These pre-built modules provide ready-made functions and tools for a wide range of automation needs, saving developers significant time and effort. Some key libraries include:

- `os` **and** `shutil`: For interacting with the operating system, managing files and directories.
- `requests`: For making HTTP requests and interacting with web services.

- `Beautiful Soup`: For web scraping and extracting data from HTML and XML.
- `Selenium`: For automating web browsers and interacting with web pages.
- `openpyxl`: For reading and writing Excel spreadsheets.
- `smtplib` **and** `imaplib`: For sending and receiving emails.
- `schedule`: For scheduling tasks and running scripts at specific times.

These are just a few examples of the many powerful libraries available in Python's automation toolkit.

3. Cross-Platform Compatibility

Python is a cross-platform language, meaning that scripts written on one operating system (e.g., Windows) can usually run without modification on other systems (e.g., macOS or Linux). This portability is a major advantage in automation, as it allows you to create scripts that work seamlessly across different environments.

4. Strong Community Support

Python has a large and active community of users and developers. This vibrant community provides ample resources, including online forums, tutorials, and documentation, making it easy to find help and support when needed. The collaborative nature of the Python community ensures that the language continues to evolve and improve, with new libraries and tools being developed constantly.

5. Versatility and Flexibility

Python is not limited to automation. It's a general-purpose language used in various domains, including web development, data science, and machine learning. This versatility allows you to leverage your Python skills for other tasks beyond automation, making it a valuable asset in your programming repertoire.

6. Scripting Capabilities

Python excels as a scripting language, allowing you to write short, powerful scripts to automate specific tasks quickly. This is particularly useful for automating routine tasks or creating small utilities to simplify your workflow.

7. Integration with Other Systems

Python can easily integrate with other systems and technologies. Whether you need to interact with databases, web services, or other applications,

Python provides the tools and libraries to connect and communicate with these systems seamlessly. This interoperability is crucial in automating complex workflows that span multiple platforms and applications.

In conclusion, Python's combination of simplicity, extensive libraries, cross-platform compatibility, strong community support, versatility, scripting capabilities, and integration capabilities makes it an ideal choice for workflow automation. Whether you're a beginner or an experienced programmer, Python provides the tools and resources you need to automate tasks effectively and boost your productivity.

Setting Up Your Python Environment

Before you embark on your Python automation journey, it's essential to set up a proper Python environment on your computer. This involves installing Python, selecting an appropriate code editor or IDE, and familiarizing yourself with the necessary tools.

1. Installing Python

The first step is to download and install the latest version of Python from the official Python website (python.org). The website provides installers for various operating systems, including Windows, macOS, and Linux. Choose the installer that corresponds to your system and follow the installation instructions.

During the installation process, ensure that you add Python to your system's PATH environment variable. This allows you to run Python commands from any directory in your terminal or command prompt.

2. Choosing a Code Editor or IDE

A code editor or Integrated Development Environment (IDE) is where you'll write and edit your Python code. Several excellent options are available, each with its own strengths and features. Some popular choices include:

- **VS Code:** A lightweight and versatile code editor with excellent Python support through extensions.
- **PyCharm:** A full-featured IDE specifically designed for Python development, offering advanced debugging and code analysis tools.
- **Sublime Text:** A fast and customizable code editor with a strong Python community.

- **Atom:** An open-source code editor developed by GitHub, known for its hackability and extensibility.

The choice of editor is largely a matter of personal preference. Experiment with different options and choose the one that best suits your workflow and needs.

3. Installing Necessary Packages

Python's strength lies in its extensive collection of libraries. To use these libraries, you need to install them into your Python environment. The most common way to install packages is using `pip`, Python's package installer.

Open your terminal or command prompt and use the following command to install a package:

Bash

```
pip install package_name
```

For example, to install the `requests` library, you would run:

Bash

```
pip install requests
```

You can also install multiple packages at once by listing their names:

Bash

```
pip   install   requests   beautifulsoup4
selenium
```

4. Using Virtual Environments (Recommended)

It's highly recommended to use virtual environments for your Python projects. A virtual environment is an isolated environment where you can install packages specific to a particular project without affecting your global Python installation or other projects.

To create a virtual environment, use the `venv` module:

Bash

```
python -m venv env_name
```

This will create a new directory named `env_name` (you can choose any name) containing a self-contained Python environment.

To activate the virtual environment:

- **On Windows:** `env_name\Scripts\activate`
- **On macOS/Linux:** `source env_name/bin/activate`

Once activated, any packages you install using `pip` will be installed within the virtual environment, keeping your projects organized and preventing conflicts between different project dependencies.

5. Exploring the Python Interpreter

The Python interpreter is an interactive shell that allows you to execute Python code line by line. It's a valuable tool for experimenting with code, testing small snippets, and exploring Python's features.

To access the interpreter, simply type `python` in your terminal or command prompt. You'll be greeted with the Python prompt (>>>), where you can start typing and executing Python code.

6. Writing Your First Python Script

Now that your environment is set up, you can start writing your first Python script. Create a new file with a `.py` extension (e.g., `my_script.py`) using your code editor.

Write some Python code in the file, for example:

Python

```python
print("Hello, world!")
```

Save the file and run it from your terminal using:

Bash

```bash
python my_script.py
```

This will execute the code in the file and print "Hello, world!" to the console.

With your Python environment configured and your first script executed, you're now ready to dive deeper into the world of Python automation. In the following chapters, we'll explore the fundamental concepts and techniques that will empower you to automate tasks and streamline your workflows.

Chapter 2: Python Basics for Automation

Data Types and Variables

In the realm of programming, data is the foundation upon which we build applications and automate tasks. Python, like any other programming language, provides a rich set of data types to represent various kinds of information. Understanding these data types is crucial for effectively manipulating and processing data within your automation scripts.

What are Data Types?

A data type defines the nature of a value and the operations that can be performed on it. Python offers several built-in data types, each serving a specific purpose:

- **Numeric Types:**
    - **Integers** (`int`): Represent whole numbers, both positive and negative (e.g., 10, -5, 0).
    - **Floating-point numbers** (`float`): Represent numbers with decimal points (e.g., 3.14, -2.5, 0.0).

- o **Complex numbers** (`complex`): Represent numbers with real and imaginary components (e.g., 2 + 3j).
- **Text Type:**
  - o **Strings** (`str`): Represent sequences of characters enclosed in single or double quotes (e.g., "Hello", 'Python').
- **Boolean Type:**
  - o **Booleans** (`bool`): Represent truth values, either `True` or `False`.
- **Sequence Types:**
  - o **Lists** (`list`): Ordered, mutable collections of items, enclosed in square brackets (e.g., [1, 2, 3], ["apple", "banana"]).
  - o **Tuples** (`tuple`): Ordered, immutable collections of items, enclosed in parentheses (e.g., (1, 2, 3), ("apple", "banana")).
  - o **Ranges** (`range`): Represent sequences of numbers, commonly used for looping.
- **Mapping Type:**
  - o **Dictionaries** (`dict`): Unordered collections of key-value pairs, enclosed in curly braces (e.g., {"name": "John", "age": 30}).
- **Set Types:**

- **Sets** (`set`): Unordered collections of unique items.
  - **Frozen sets** (`frozenset`): Immutable versions of sets.
- **Binary Types:**
  - **Bytes** (`bytes`): Sequences of bytes, representing raw data.
  - **Byte arrays** (`bytearray`): Mutable versions of bytes.
- **None Type:**
  - `None`: Represents the absence of a value.

Variables: Storing Data

Variables are named containers that hold data values. They act as symbolic representations of data, allowing us to refer to and manipulate values by their names.

Variable Assignment

In Python, we assign values to variables using the assignment operator (`=`):

Python

```python
name = "Alice"
age = 30
price = 19.99
```

```
is_student = True
```

This code creates four variables (`name`, `age`, `price`, and `is_student`) and assigns them values of different data types.

Variable Naming Rules

When naming variables, adhere to these rules:

- Variable names must start with a letter or underscore.
- Variable names can contain letters, numbers, and underscores.
- Variable names are case-sensitive[1] (`my_variable` is different from `My_Variable`).
- Choose descriptive names that reflect the purpose of the variable.

Using Variables in Automation

Variables play a crucial role in automation scripts. They allow you to store data, perform calculations, and make decisions based on the values they hold.

For example, in a script that automates email sending, you might use variables to store the recipient's email address, the subject of the email, and the email body.

Data Type Conversion

Sometimes, you may need to convert data from one type to another. Python provides built-in functions for type conversion:

- `int()`: Converts a value to an integer.
- `float()`: Converts a value to a floating-point number.
- `str()`: Converts a[2] value to a string.
- `bool()`: Converts a value to a boolean.
- `list()`: Converts a value to a list.
- `tuple()`: Converts a value to a tuple.
- `dict()`: Converts a value to a dictionary.
- `set()`: Converts a value to a set.[3]

Example:

Python

```
price = "19.99"   # price is a string
numeric_price = float(price)    # convert
price to a float
```

Understanding data types and variables is fundamental to writing effective Python scripts. By mastering these concepts, you'll be well-equipped to manipulate data, perform calculations, and automate tasks with precision and efficiency.

Operators and Expressions

In Python, operators are special symbols that perform operations on data. They allow you to manipulate values, perform calculations, and make comparisons. Expressions combine operators and operands (values) to produce a new value. Mastering operators and expressions is essential for writing effective Python automation scripts.

Arithmetic Operators

Arithmetic operators perform basic mathematical operations:

- + **(Addition):** Adds two operands.
- − **(Subtraction):** Subtracts the second operand from the first.
- * **(Multiplication):** Multiplies[1] two operands.
- / **(Division):** Divides the first operand by the second.

- **%** **(Modulo):** Returns the remainder of[2] the division.
- ****** **(Exponentiation):** Raises the first operand to the power of the second.
- **//** **(Floor Division):** Returns the quotient of the division,[3] rounded down to the nearest integer.

Example:

Python

```
x = 10
y = 3

sum = x + y   # 13
difference = x - y   # 7
product = x * y   # 30
quotient = x / y   # 3.3333333333333335
remainder = x % y   # 1
power = x ** y   # 1000
floor_division = x // y   # 3
```

Comparison Operators

Comparison operators compare two values and return a boolean result (True or False):

- == **(Equal to):** Checks if[4] two operands are equal.
- != **(Not equal to):** Checks if two operands are not equal.
- > **(Greater than):** Checks if the first operand is greater than the second.[5]
- < **(Less than):** Checks if the first operand is less than the second.
- >= **(Greater than or equal to):** Checks if the first operand is greater than or equal to the second.
- <= **(Less than or equal to):** Checks if the first operand is less than or equal to the second.[6]

Example:

Python

```
x = 10
y = 3

is_equal = x == y   # False
is_not_equal = x != y   # True
is_greater = x > y   # True
is_less = x < y   # False
```

Logical Operators

Logical operators combine boolean values:

- and **(Logical AND):** Returns True if both operands are True.
- or **(Logical OR):** Returns True if at least one operand is True.
- not **(Logical NOT):** Returns the opposite of the operand's[7] boolean value.

Example:

Python

```python
x = True
y = False

result_and = x and y   # False
result_or = x or y    # True
result_not_x = not x   # False
result_not_y = not y   # True
```

Assignment Operators

Assignment operators combine assignment with arithmetic or bitwise operations:

- `=` **(Assign):** Assigns the value of the right operand to the left operand.
- `+=` **(Add and assign):** Adds the right operand to the left operand and assigns the result to the left operand.
- `-=` **(Subtract and[8] assign):** Subtracts the right operand from the left operand and assigns the result to the left operand.
- `*=` **(Multiply and assign):** Multiplies the left operand by the right operand and assigns the result to the left operand.
- `/=` **(Divide and assign):** Divides the left operand by the right operand and assigns the result to the left operand.
- `%=` **(Modulo and assign):**[9] Calculates the modulo of the left operand by the right operand and assigns the result to the left operand.
- `**=` **(Exponentiate and assign):** Raises the left operand to the power of the right operand and assigns the result to the left operand.[10]
- `//=` **(Floor divide and assign):** Performs floor division on the left operand by the right operand and assigns the result to the left operand.[11]

Example:

Python

```
x = 10
x += 5  # x is now 15
x -= 3  # x is now 12
```

Bitwise Operators

Bitwise operators perform operations on the binary representations of integers. These are less commonly used in basic automation but are essential for certain tasks, like working with low-level hardware or network protocols.

Operator Precedence

Python follows a specific order of operations when evaluating expressions. This is known as operator precedence. Parentheses can be used to override the default precedence and force certain operations to be evaluated first.

Expressions in Automation

Expressions are used extensively in automation scripts to perform calculations, make comparisons, and manipulate data. For example, you might use an expression to calculate the total price of items in a shopping cart, determine if a file size exceeds a certain limit, or extract specific information from a string.

By understanding operators and expressions, you gain the ability to perform a wide range of operations on data within your automation scripts. This knowledge is fundamental for creating dynamic and powerful automation solutions.

Control Flow (if/else, loops)

In the world of programming, controlling the flow of execution is crucial. It allows us to dictate the order in which instructions are carried out, making our programs dynamic and responsive to different conditions. Python provides powerful control flow structures, such as `if/else` statements and loops, that enable us to create intelligent automation scripts capable of making decisions and repeating actions.

Conditional Statements: `if/else`

`if/else` statements allow us to execute different blocks of code based on certain conditions. The basic structure of an `if/else` statement is as follows:

Python

```
if condition:
    # Code to execute if the condition is
True
else:
    # Code to execute if the condition is
False[1]
```

The `condition` is an expression that evaluates to either `True` or `False`. If the condition is `True`, the code[2] block indented under the `if` statement is executed. If the condition is `False`, the code block[3] indented under the `else` statement (if present) is executed.

Example:

Python

```
age = 20

if age >= 18:
    print("You are eligible to vote.")
else:
    print("You are not yet eligible to
vote.")
```

In this example, the code checks if the `age` variable is greater than or equal to 18. If it is, the message "You are eligible to vote." is printed. Otherwise, the message "You are not yet eligible to vote." is printed.

`elif` Clause

We can use the `elif` clause to check multiple conditions:

Python

```python
score = 85

if score >= 90:
  print("Grade: A")
elif score >= 80:
  print("Grade: B")
elif score >= 70:
  print("Grade: C")
else:
  print("Grade: D")
```

This code assigns a letter grade based on the value of the `score` variable.

Nested `if/else`

`if/else` statements can be nested within each other to create more complex decision-making logic:

Python

```
x = 10
y = 5

if x > y:
  if x % 2 == 0:
      print("x is greater than y and is even.")
  else:
      print("x is greater than y and is odd.")
else:
  print("x is not greater than y.")
```

Loops: `for` **and** `while`

Loops allow us to repeat a block of code multiple times. Python provides two main types of loops: `for` loops and `while` loops.

`for` **Loop**

A `for` loop iterates over a sequence (e.g., a list, tuple, string, or range) and executes the code block for each item in the sequence.

Python

```
fruits = ["apple", "banana", "cherry"]

for fruit in fruits:
  print(fruit)
```

This code prints each fruit in the `fruits` list.

`while` **Loop**

A `while` loop continues to execute the code block as long as a certain condition remains `True`.

Python

```
count = 0
```

```
while count < 5:
  print(count)
  count += 1
```

This code prints the numbers from 0 to 4.

`break` and `continue` Statements

The `break` statement terminates the loop prematurely. The `continue` statement skips the current iteration and proceeds to the next one.

Example:

Python

```
for i in range(10):
  if i == 5:
    break  # Exit the loop when i is 5
  print(i)

for i in range(10):
  if i % 2 == 0:
    continue  # Skip even numbers
  print(i)
```
[4]

Loops in Automation

Loops are invaluable in automation for tasks that involve repetition. For instance, you can use a loop to process a list of files, send emails to multiple recipients, or perform calculations on a dataset.

By mastering control flow structures like `if/else` statements and loops, you gain the ability to create dynamic and responsive automation scripts that can adapt to different situations and perform complex tasks efficiently.

Chapter 3: Working with Files and Data

File Input and Output

File handling is a fundamental aspect of many automation tasks. Whether you need to read data from a configuration file, process a CSV dataset, or generate reports, interacting with files is essential. Python provides a robust set of tools for file input and output (I/O) operations, allowing you to seamlessly work with various file formats.

Opening Files

Before you can read from or write to a file, you need to open it. Python's built-in `open()` function provides a way to access files. The basic syntax is:

Python

```
file_object = open(filename, mode)
```

- `filename`: The name of the file you want to open (including the path if it's not in the current directory).
- `mode`: A string specifying how you want to open the file. Common modes include:

- ○ `'r'`: Read mode (default). Opens the file for reading.
- ○ `'w'`: Write mode. Opens the file for writing, creating a new file if it doesn't exist or overwriting it if it does.
- ○ `'a'`: Append mode. Opens the file for writing, appending data to the end of the file if it exists.
- ○ `'x'`: Create mode. Creates a new file and opens it for writing.
- ○ `'t'`: Text mode (default). Opens the file for reading or writing text data.
- ○ `'b'`: Binary mode. Opens the file for reading or writing binary data.

Example:

Python

```
# Open a file for reading
file_object = open('my_file.txt', 'r')

# Open a file for writing
file_object = open('output.txt', 'w')
```

Reading from Files

Once a file is opened in read mode, you can read its contents using various methods:

- `read()`: Reads the entire file content as a single string.
- `readline()`: Reads a single line from the file.
- `readlines()`: Reads all lines from the file and returns them as a list of strings.[1]

Example:

Python

```
file_object = open('my_file.txt', 'r')

# Read the entire file content
content = file_object.read()
print(content)

# Read a single line
line = file_object.readline()
print(line)

# Read all lines into a list
lines = file_object.readlines()
for line in lines:
  print(line)

file_object.close()
```

Writing to Files

To write data to a file, open it in write (`'w'`) or append (`'a'`) mode. Use the `write()` method to write data to the file.

Example:

Python

```python
file_object = open('output.txt', 'w')

file_object.write("This     is     the     first
line.\n")
file_object.write("This     is     the     second
line.\n")

file_object.close()
```

Closing Files

It's crucial to close files after you're done with them using the `close()` method. This releases the file resources and ensures that any data written to the file is properly saved.

Python

```
file_object.close()
```

Using the `with` Statement

A more convenient way to handle files is using the `with` statement. This ensures that the file is automatically closed even if an error occurs.

Python

```
with     open('my_file.txt',     'r')     as
file_object:
  content = file_object.read()
  print(content)
```

Working with Different File Formats

Python provides modules for working with specific file formats:

- **CSV Files:** The `csv` module provides functions for reading and writing CSV (Comma Separated Values) files.

- **JSON Files:** The `json` module allows you to work with JSON (JavaScript Object Notation) data.
- **Excel Files:** The `openpyxl` library enables you to read and write Excel spreadsheets.

These are just a few examples. Python's rich ecosystem offers libraries for handling various other file formats, including XML, PDF, and image files.

By mastering file I/O operations, you gain the ability to interact with external data sources, process information stored in files, and generate reports. This is a crucial skill for automating tasks that involve data manipulation and analysis.

Reading and Writing CSV Files

CSV (Comma Separated Values) files are a common format for storing tabular data. They are simple text files where each line represents a row, and values within a row are separated by commas. Python's `csv` module provides powerful tools for reading and writing CSV files, making it easy to process and manipulate data stored in this format.

Reading CSV Files

To read a CSV file, you first need to import the `csv` module. Then, use the `csv.reader()` function to create a reader object that iterates over the rows in the file.

Python

```python
import csv

with open('data.csv', 'r') as file:
    reader = csv.reader(file)
    for row in reader:
        print(row)
```

This code opens the `data.csv` file in read mode and creates a reader object. The `for` loop iterates over each row in the file, printing it to the console. Each `row` is a list of strings, where each string represents a value in that row.

Accessing Specific Values

You can access individual values within a row by their index. For example, to access the first value in a row:

Python

```python
first_value = row[0]
```

Handling Header Rows

Many CSV files have a header row that defines the names of the columns. You can use the `next()` function to skip the header row:

Python

```python
import csv

with open('data.csv', 'r') as file:
    reader = csv.reader(file)
    next(reader)   # Skip the header row
    for row in reader:
        print(row)
```

Using `DictReader`

For easier access to values by column names, you can use `csv.DictReader()`. This creates a reader object that returns each row as a dictionary, where keys are the column names (from the header row) and values are the corresponding values in that row.

Python

```python
import csv

with open('data.csv', 'r') as file:
    reader = csv.DictReader(file)
    for row in reader:
        print(row['Name'], row['Age'])   # Access values by column name
```

Writing CSV Files

To write data to a CSV file, use the `csv.writer()` function to create a writer object. Then, use the `writerow()` method to write individual rows to the file.

Python

```python
import csv

data = [
    ['Name', 'Age', 'City'],
    ['Alice', '30', 'New York'],
    ['Bob', '25', 'Los Angeles'],
```

```
]
with open('output.csv', 'w', newline='') as
file:
    writer = csv.writer(file)
    writer.writerows(data)   # Write multiple
rows at once
```

This code creates a CSV file named `output.csv` and writes the data from the `data` list to the file. The `newline=''` argument is used to prevent extra blank lines from being added to the file.

Using `DictWriter`

Similar to `DictReader`, you can use `csv.DictWriter()` to write data to a CSV file using dictionaries.

Python

```
import csv

data = [
    {'Name': 'Alice', 'Age': '30', 'City':
'New York'},
    {'Name': 'Bob', 'Age': '25', 'City': 'Los
Angeles'},
```

```
]
with open('output.csv', 'w', newline='') as
file:
    fieldnames = ['Name', 'Age', 'City']
        writer    =    csv.DictWriter(file,
fieldnames=fieldnames)
    writer.writeheader()   # Write[1] the header
row
    writer.writerows(data)
```

This code writes the data from the `data` list of dictionaries to the CSV file, including a header row with the specified field names.

Customizing CSV Output

The `csv` module provides options for customizing the output, such as changing the delimiter (the character used to separate values) or the quote character.

Example:

Python

```
import csv
```

```
with open('output.csv', 'w', newline='') as
file:
    writer = csv.writer(file, delimiter=';',
quotechar='"')
    # ... write data ...
```

This code uses a semicolon (;) as the delimiter and a double quote (") as the quote character.

By mastering the techniques for reading and writing CSV files, you gain a valuable tool for automating tasks that involve data extraction, transformation, and loading (ETL). This is essential for working with datasets, generating reports, and integrating with other systems that use the CSV format.

Handling Excel Spreadsheets with `openpyxl`

Excel spreadsheets are ubiquitous in business and data analysis. Automating tasks involving Excel files can save significant time and reduce errors. The `openpyxl` library provides a powerful way to interact with Excel spreadsheets in Python, allowing you to read, write, and manipulate data within these files.

Installation

Before you can use `openpyxl`, you need to install it using `pip`:

Bash

```
pip install openpyxl
```

Opening an Excel File

To work with an Excel file, you first need to open it using `openpyxl.load_workbook()`:

Python

```
from openpyxl import load_workbook

workbook =
load_workbook('my_spreadsheet.xlsx')
```

This code opens the `my_spreadsheet.xlsx` file and creates a workbook object.

Accessing Worksheets

An Excel workbook can contain multiple worksheets. You can access a specific worksheet by its name:

Python

```
worksheet = workbook['Sheet1']
```

Or you can access the active worksheet:

Python

```
worksheet = workbook.active
```

Reading Data from Cells

You can access the value of a cell using its coordinates (e.g., A1, B2):

Python

```
cell_value = worksheet['A1'].value
print(cell_value)
```

Iterating over Rows and Columns

To iterate over rows or columns, you can use `worksheet.iter_rows()` or `worksheet.iter_cols()`:

Python

```python
# Iterate over rows
for row in worksheet.iter_rows():
  for cell in row:
    print(cell.value)

# Iterate over columns
for col in worksheet.iter_cols():
  for cell in col:
    print(cell.value)
```

You can specify the range of rows or columns to iterate over using the `min_row`, `max_row`, `min_col`, and `max_col` arguments.

Example:

Python

```python
# Iterate over rows 2 to 5 and columns 1 to 3
for row in worksheet.iter_rows(min_row=2, max_row=5, min_col=1, max_col=3):
  for cell in row:
    print(cell.value)
```

Writing Data to Cells

You can write data to a cell by assigning a value to its coordinate:

Python

```python
worksheet['A1'] = 'New Value'
```

Adding Rows and Columns

You can add rows or columns using `worksheet.insert_rows()` and `worksheet.insert_cols()`:

Python

```python
# Insert a row at row 4
worksheet.insert_rows(4)

# Insert a column at column 2
worksheet.insert_cols(2)
```

Deleting Rows and Columns

Similarly, you can delete rows or columns using `worksheet.delete_rows()` and `worksheet.delete_cols()`:

Python

```python
# Delete row 3
worksheet.delete_rows(3)

# Delete column 2
worksheet.delete_cols(2)
```

Saving Changes

After making changes to the workbook, remember to save them using `workbook.save()`:

Python

```python
workbook.save('my_spreadsheet.xlsx')
```

Formatting Cells

`openpyxl` allows you to format cells, including changing font styles, colors, and alignment.

Example:

Python

```python
from openpyxl.styles import Font

cell = worksheet['A1']
cell.font = Font(bold=True, color='FF0000')
# Red bold font
```

Working with Formulas

You can also work with formulas in Excel using `openpyxl`.

Example:

Python

```
worksheet['C1'] = '=SUM(A1:B1)'
```

This code inserts a formula in cell `C1` that calculates the sum of the values in cells `A1` and `B1`.

By exploring these features, you can automate a wide range of tasks involving Excel spreadsheets, from data entry and cleaning to report generation and analysis. This makes `openpyxl` a valuable tool for anyone working with Excel data in Python.

Part II: Automating Common Tasks and Processes

Chapter 4: Automating Web Tasks

Web Scraping with `Beautiful Soup`

The internet is a vast repository of information, and often, we need to extract specific data from websites for analysis, research, or automation. Web scraping is the process of automatically extracting data from websites. While there are various approaches to web scraping, Python's `Beautiful Soup` library stands out for its simplicity and effectiveness in parsing HTML and XML documents, making it a popular choice for web scraping tasks.

Installation

Before you can use `Beautiful Soup`, you need to install it using `pip`:

Bash

```
pip install beautifulsoup4
```

Making a Request

To scrape data from a website, you first need to fetch the website's HTML content. The `requests` library is commonly used for this purpose.

Python

```python
import requests

url = 'https://www.example.com'
response = requests.get(url)
html_content = response.text
```

This code sends a GET request to the specified URL and retrieves the HTML content of the webpage.

Parsing the HTML

Once you have the HTML content, you can use `Beautiful Soup` to parse it and extract the desired information.

Python

```python
from bs4 import BeautifulSoup

soup      =      BeautifulSoup(html_content,
'html.parser')
```

This code creates a `Beautiful Soup` object (`soup`) that represents the parsed HTML structure. The `'html.parser'` argument specifies the parser to use.

Finding Elements

`Beautiful Soup` provides various methods for finding elements within the HTML:

- `find()`: Returns the first matching element.
- `find_all()`: Returns a list of all matching elements.

You can search for elements by tag name, attributes, or text content.

Example:

Python

```python
# Find all paragraph elements
paragraphs = soup.find_all('p')

# Find the first div element with class
"content"
content_div          =          soup.find('div',
class_='content')
```

```
# Find all links with text "Read more"
read_more_links    =    soup.find_all('a',
text='Read more')
```

Extracting Data

Once you have found the relevant elements, you can extract data from them:

- `text`: Returns the text content of an element.
- `get('attribute')`: Returns the value of a specific attribute.

Example:

Python

```
# Extract text from a paragraph
paragraph_text = paragraphs[0].text

# Extract the href attribute from a link
link_url = read_more_links[0].get('href')
```

Navigating the HTML Tree

Beautiful Soup allows you to navigate the HTML tree structure using attributes like parent, children, next_sibling, and previous_sibling.

Example:

Python

```
# Find the parent element of a paragraph
parent_element = paragraphs[0].parent

# Find all child elements of a div
child_elements = content_div.children
```

Handling Errors

Web scraping can be prone to errors, such as network issues or changes in website structure. It's essential to handle these errors gracefully using try-except blocks.

Example:

Python

```
import requests
from bs4 import BeautifulSoup
```

```
url = 'https://www.example.com'

try:
  response = requests.get(url)
    response.raise_for_status()    # Raise an
exception for bad status codes
      soup  =  BeautifulSoup(response.text,
'html.parser')
  # ... extract data ...
except  requests.exceptions.RequestException
as e:
  print(f"Error fetching URL: {e}")
except Exception as e:
  print(f"An error occurred: {e}")
```

Ethical Considerations

When scraping websites, it's important to be
mindful of ethical considerations:

- **Respect robots.txt:** Check the website's
  `robots.txt` file to see if web scraping is
  allowed.
- **Avoid overloading the server:** Make
  requests at a reasonable rate to avoid
  overloading the website's server.

- **Use the data responsibly:** Ensure you comply with any terms of service or usage restrictions.

Advanced Techniques

`Beautiful Soup` can be combined with other libraries and techniques for more advanced web scraping:

- **Selenium:** For scraping dynamic websites that rely on JavaScript.
- **Scrapy:** A powerful web scraping framework for building scalable scrapers.

By mastering `Beautiful Soup` and adhering to ethical practices, you can effectively extract data from websites for various automation tasks, such as data analysis, price monitoring, and content aggregation.

Interacting with APIs

Modern web applications often expose their functionality through Application Programming Interfaces (APIs). APIs allow different software systems to communicate and exchange data with each[1] other. In the context of automation, interacting with APIs is crucial for accessing data, triggering actions, and integrating with external services. Python, with its rich ecosystem of libraries, makes it easy to interact with various APIs.

Understanding APIs

An API defines a set of rules and specifications that govern how software components or systems interact. It acts as an intermediary between different applications, allowing them to exchange data and functionality. APIs typically use the HTTP protocol for communication, with requests and responses often formatted in JSON or XML.

Making API Requests

The `requests` library is a powerful tool for making HTTP requests to APIs. You can use it to send various types of requests, including:

- **GET:** Retrieve data from an API endpoint.
- **POST:** Send data to an API endpoint to create or update a resource.
- **PUT:** Update an existing resource.
- **DELETE:** Delete a resource.

Example (GET request):

Python

```python
import requests

url = 'https://api.example.com/data'
response = requests.get(url)

# Check the status code
if response.status_code == 200:
    data = response.json()   # Parse the JSON
response
    print(data)
else:
    print(f"Error: {response.status_code}")
```

This code sends a GET request to the specified API endpoint and retrieves the data in JSON format.

Authentication

Many APIs require authentication to access their resources. Common authentication methods include:

- **API keys:** Unique identifiers that grant access to the API.
- **OAuth:** A protocol that allows users to grant third-party applications access to their resources without sharing their credentials.[2]

Example (API key):

Python

```
import requests

url = 'https://api.example.com/data'
api_key = 'YOUR_API_KEY'
headers    =    {'Authorization':    f'Bearer
{api_key}'}
response         =           requests.get(url,
headers=headers)
```

This code includes the API key in the request headers to authenticate the request.

Handling Responses

API responses typically come in JSON or XML format. Python provides libraries for parsing these formats:

- **JSON:** Use the `json` module to parse JSON responses.
- **XML:** Use the `xml.etree.ElementTree` module to parse XML responses.

Example (JSON response):

Python

```python
import requests

url = 'https://api.example.com/data'
response = requests.get(url)

if response.status_code == 200:
    data = response.json()[3]
    # Access data elements
    name = data['name']
    age = data['age']
    print(f"Name: {name}, Age: {age}")
```

Error Handling

API requests can encounter errors, such as network issues, invalid requests, or server errors. It's crucial to handle these errors gracefully using `try-except` blocks and checking the response status code.

Example:

Python

```python
import requests
```

```
url = 'https://api.example.com/data'

try:
    response = requests.get(url)
    response.raise_for_status()    # Raise an
exception for bad status codes
    # ... process the response ...
except requests.exceptions.RequestException
as e:
    print(f"Error: {e}")
```

Rate Limiting

Many APIs have rate limits that restrict the number of requests you can make within a specific time frame. Exceeding these limits can result in your[4] requests being blocked. It's essential to be aware of rate limits and implement strategies to handle them, such as adding delays between requests or using caching mechanisms.

API Documentation

API providers typically offer documentation that outlines the available endpoints, request parameters, response formats, and authentication methods. Refer to the API documentation to understand how to interact with the API correctly.

By mastering the techniques for interacting with APIs, you can automate a wide range of tasks, such as retrieving data from web services, integrating with social media platforms, controlling smart home devices, and automating business processes. This opens up a world of possibilities for building powerful and efficient automation solutions.

Browser Automation with `Selenium`

While `Beautiful Soup` excels at parsing static HTML content, many websites rely heavily on JavaScript for dynamic content and user interactions. To automate tasks on such websites, you need a tool that can control a web browser and interact with its elements just like a human user would. This is where `Selenium` comes in. `Selenium` is a powerful framework for automating web browsers, enabling you to perform actions like clicking buttons, filling forms, navigating pages, and extracting data from dynamic content.

Installation

First, install the `selenium` package using `pip`:

Bash

```
pip install selenium
```

You'll also need to download a WebDriver specific to the browser you want to automate. WebDrivers are browser-specific drivers that allow `Selenium` to control the browser. You can find WebDrivers for Chrome, Firefox, Edge, and other browsers on their respective websites.

Setting Up the WebDriver

Once you have downloaded the WebDriver, you need to tell `Selenium` where to find it. You can either add the WebDriver's location to your system's PATH environment variable or specify the path directly in your code.

Example (specifying the path in code):

Python

```
from selenium import webdriver

# Path to the ChromeDriver executable
driver_path = '/path/to/chromedriver'
```

```
# Create a Chrome WebDriver instance
driver                              =
webdriver.Chrome(executable_path=driver_pat
h)
```

Opening a Webpage

To open a webpage in the browser, use the
`driver.get()` method:

Python

```
url = 'https://www.example.com'
driver.get(url)
```

Finding Elements

`Selenium` provides various methods for finding
elements on a webpage:

- `find_element_by_id()`: Finds an element
  by its ID attribute.

- `find_element_by_name()`: Finds an element by its name attribute.
- `find_element_by_class_name()`: Finds an element by its class name.
- `find_element_by_tag_name()`: Finds an element by its tag name.
- `find_element_by_css_selector()`: Finds an element using a CSS selector.
- `find_element_by_xpath()`: Finds an element using an XPath expression.

These methods return a single WebElement object. To find multiple elements, use the corresponding `find_elements_by_*()` methods, which return a list of WebElements.

Example:

Python

```
# Find the search input field by its name
attribute
search_input                           =
driver.find_element_by_name('q')

# Find all links on the page
links                                  =
driver.find_elements_by_tag_name('a')
```

Interacting with Elements

Once you have found an element, you can interact with it using various methods:

- `click()`: Clicks the element (e.g., a button or link).
- `send_keys()`: Sends text to the element (e.g., typing in an input field).
- `clear()`: Clears the content of the element (e.g., an input field).
- `submit()`: Submits a form.

Example:

Python

```python
# Type "Selenium" into the search input field
search_input.send_keys('Selenium')

# Submit the search form
search_input.submit()
```

Navigating Pages

You can navigate between pages using these methods:

- `back()`: Goes back to the previous page.
- `forward()`: Goes forward to the next page.
- `refresh()`: Refreshes the current page.

Waiting for Elements

Sometimes, you need to wait for an element to load before interacting with it. `Selenium` provides explicit waits for this purpose:

Python

```python
from selenium.webdriver.common.by import By
from selenium.webdriver.support.ui import WebDriverWait
from selenium.webdriver.support import expected_conditions as EC[1]

# Wait for up to 10 seconds for an element
with ID "my_element" to be present
element = WebDriverWait(driver, 10).until(
    EC.presence_of_element_located((By.ID,
'my_element'))
)
```

Executing JavaScript

You can execute JavaScript code in the browser using `driver.execute_script()`:

Python

```
# Scroll to the bottom of the page
driver.execute_script("window.scrollTo(0,
document.body.scrollHeight);")
```

Closing the Browser

When you're finished with the browser, close it using `driver.quit()`:

Python

```
driver.quit()
```

Advanced Techniques

`Selenium` offers many other features, including:

- Handling alerts and pop-up windows
- Taking screenshots
- Working with cookies
- Using headless browsers (browsers without a graphical user interface)

By exploring these features and combining `Selenium` with other libraries like `Beautiful Soup`, you can automate a wide range of web tasks, such as web testing, data extraction, form submission, and social media interaction.

Chapter 5: Automating System Administration

System administration often involves repetitive tasks like managing files, running programs, and monitoring system resources. Python, with its OS-related modules, provides a powerful platform for automating these tasks, allowing system administrators to improve efficiency, reduce errors, and free up time for more strategic work.

The `os` Module

The `os` module is a cornerstone of Python's system administration capabilities. It provides functions for interacting with the operating system, including:

- **File and Directory Manipulation:**
    - `os.getcwd()`: Get the current working directory.
    - `os.chdir(path)`: Change the current working directory.
    - `os.listdir(path)`: List files and directories in a given path.
    - `os.mkdir(path)`: Create a new directory.

- ○ `os.makedirs(path)`: Create a directory and any necessary intermediate directories.
- ○ `os.rename(src, dst)`: Rename a file or directory.
- ○ `os.remove(path)`: Remove a file.
- ○ `os.rmdir(path)`: Remove an empty directory.
- ○ `os.removedirs(path)`: Remove a directory and any empty parent directories.
- ○ `os.path.exists(path)`: Check if a file or directory exists.
- ○ `os.path.isfile(path)`: Check if a path is a file.
- ○ `os.path.isdir(path)`: Check if a path is a directory.
- ○ `os.path.join(path1, path2, ...)`: Join multiple path components.

Example:

Python

```
import os

# Get the current working directory
current_directory = os.getcwd()
```

```
print(f"Current                  directory:
{current_directory}")[1]

# Create a new directory
os.mkdir('new_directory')

# List files in the current directory
files = os.listdir('.')
print(f"Files: {files}")
```

Running External Programs

The `os` module allows you to run external programs using the `os.system()` function:

Python

```
os.system('ls -l')    # Run the 'ls -l'
command
```

However, for more control over the execution of external programs, the `subprocess` module is recommended.

The `subprocess` Module

The `subprocess` module provides a more flexible and powerful way to run external programs and interact with their input/output.

- `subprocess.run()`: Runs an external command and waits for it to complete.
- `subprocess.Popen()`: Creates a new process and allows you to interact with its input/output streams.

Example (`subprocess.run()`):

Python

```
import subprocess

result = subprocess.run(['ls', '-l'],
capture_output=True, text=True)
print(result.stdout)
```

This code runs the `ls -l` command and captures its output.

Environment Variables

The `os` module also provides functions for working with environment variables:

- `os.environ`: A dictionary-like object containing environment variables.
- `os.getenv(key)`: Get the value of an environment variable.
- `os.putenv(key, value)`: Set the value of an environment variable.

Example:

Python

```
import os

# Get the value of the PATH environment
variable
path_value = os.getenv('PATH')
print(f"PATH: {path_value}")
```

Working with Paths

The `os.path` submodule provides functions for working with file and directory paths:

- `os.path.abspath(path)`: Get the absolute path of a relative path.
- `os.path.basename(path)`: Get the base name of a path.
- `os.path.dirname(path)`: Get the directory name of a path.
- `os.path.split(path)`: Split a path into directory and file name components.
- `os.path.splitext(path)`: Split a path into base name and extension.

Example:

Python

```python
import os

path = 'documents/my_file.txt'
absolute_path = os.path.abspath(path)
print(f"Absolute path: {absolute_path}")

base_name = os.path.basename(path)
print(f"Base name: {base_name}")
```

Platform-Specific Operations

The `os` module provides functions for performing platform-specific operations, such as:

- `os.name`: Get the name of the operating system.
- `os.uname()`: Get system information (Unix-like systems).

Example:

Python

```python
import os

if os.name == 'posix':
  # Unix-like system
  system_info = os.uname()
  print(f"System: {system_info}")
elif os.name == 'nt':
  # Windows system
  print("Windows system")
```

By mastering the `os` and `subprocess` modules, system administrators can automate a wide range of tasks, including file management, program execution, system monitoring, and user management. This can significantly improve efficiency and reduce the burden of manual administrative work.

Managing Files and Directories

Efficient file and directory management is crucial for maintaining an organized and reliable system. Python's `os` and `shutil` modules provide a comprehensive set of tools for automating file and directory operations, enabling system administrators to perform tasks like creating, deleting, moving, copying, and organizing files and directories with ease.

File and Directory Operations with `os`

The `os` module offers a wide range of functions for interacting with the file system:

- **Creating Directories:**
  - `os.mkdir(path)`: Creates a single directory.
  - `os.makedirs(path, exist_ok=True)`: Creates a directory and any necessary intermediate directories. The `exist_ok=True` argument prevents an error if the directory already exists.

Example:

Python

```
import os

# Create a directory named 'data'
os.mkdir('data')

# Create a nested directory structure
os.makedirs('data/reports/2024',
exist_ok=True)
```

- **Listing Directory Contents:**
  - ○ `os.listdir(path)`: Returns a list of all files and directories within a given path.

Example:

Python

```
import os

# List files and directories in the current
directory
contents = os.listdir('.')
print(contents)
```

- **Removing Files and Directories:**
  - `os.remove(path)`: Deletes a file.
  - `os.rmdir(path)`: Deletes an empty directory.
  - `os.removedirs(path)`: Deletes a directory and any empty parent directories.

Example:

Python

```
import os

# Delete a file named 'old_data.txt'
os.remove('old_data.txt')

# Delete an empty directory named 'temp'
os.rmdir('temp')
```

- **Renaming and Moving Files and Directories:**
  - `os.rename(src, dst)`: Renames a file or directory from `src` to `dst`.
  - `os.replace(src, dst)`: Renames a file or directory from `src` to `dst`, overwriting the destination if it exists.

- ○ `shutil.move(src, dst)`: Moves a file or directory from `src` to `dst`.

Example:

Python

```
import os
import shutil

# Rename a file
os.rename('old_name.txt', 'new_name.txt')

# Move a file to a different directory
shutil.move('data.txt',[1] 'archive/data.txt')
```

Working with File Paths

The `os.path` submodule provides functions for manipulating file paths:

- **Joining Paths:**
  - ○ `os.path.join(path1, path2, ...)`: Joins multiple path components into a single path, handling platform-specific path separators correctly.

Example:

Python

```
import os

data_dir = 'data'
file_name = 'report.txt'
file_path      =      os.path.join(data_dir,
file_name)
print(file_path)   # Output: data/report.txt
(or data\report.txt on Windows)
```

- **Splitting Paths:**
  - `os.path.split(path)`: Splits a path into a tuple containing the directory name and the file name.
  - `os.path.splitext(path)`: Splits a path into a tuple containing the base name and the extension.

Example:

Python

```
import os

file_path = '/path/to/my_file.txt'
directory,              file_name              =
os.path.split(file_path)
print(directory)   # Output: /path/to
print(file_name)   # Output: my_file.txt
```

```
base_name,              extension              =
os.path.splitext(file_path)
print(base_name)                #        Output:
/path/to/my_file
print(extension)   # Output: .txt
```

Advanced File Operations with `shutil`

The `shutil` module provides additional functions for advanced file operations:

- **Copying Files and Directories:**
    - `shutil.copy(src, dst)`: Copies a file from `src` to `dst`.
    - `shutil.copy2(src, dst)`: Copies a file from `src` to `dst`, preserving metadata like timestamps.
    - `shutil.copytree(src, dst)`: Copies an entire directory tree from `src` to `dst`.

Example:

Python

```
import shutil
```

```
# Copy a file
shutil.copy('data.txt', 'backup/data.txt')

# Copy a directory tree
shutil.copytree('reports',
'archive/reports')
```

- **Working with Archives:**
  - `shutil.make_archive(base_name, format, root_dir)`: Creates an archive file (e.g., zip, tar) of a directory.
  - `shutil.unpack_archive(filename, extract_dir)`: Extracts an archive file.

Example:

Python

```
import shutil

# Create a zip archive of the 'reports'
directory
shutil.make_archive('reports',       'zip',
'reports')

# Extract a zip archive named 'archive.zip'
```

```
shutil.unpack_archive('archive.zip',
'extracted_archive')
```

By combining the capabilities of the `os` and `shutil` modules, system administrators can automate a wide range of file and directory management tasks, improving productivity and ensuring consistency in file system operations.

Scheduling Tasks with `schedule`

In system administration, many tasks need to be performed regularly, such as backups, log rotations, or report generation. Manually executing these tasks can be tedious and error-prone. Fortunately, Python offers libraries like `schedule` that simplify task scheduling, allowing you to automate recurring tasks with ease.

Installation

To use the `schedule` library, install it using `pip`:

Bash

```
pip install schedule
```

Scheduling Tasks

The `schedule` library provides a straightforward way to schedule tasks at specific intervals or times. You define the task you want to run and then schedule it using methods like:

- `every(interval)`: Schedules a task to run at a specified interval (e.g., every hour, every day, every week).
- `at(time_string)`: Schedules a task to run at a specific time (e.g., "10:30", "13:15").

Example (running a task every hour):

Python

```python
import schedule
import time

def job():
  print("Running hourly task...")
  # Perform your task here

schedule.every().hour.do(job)

while True:
  schedule.run_pending()
```

```
time.sleep(1)
```

This code defines a function `job()` that prints a message (you would replace this with your actual task). It then schedules this function to run every hour using `schedule.every().hour.do(job)`. The `while` loop continuously checks for pending tasks and runs them.

Scheduling with Specific Times

You can schedule tasks to run at specific times using the `at()` method:

Python

```
import schedule
import time

def job():
  print("Running task at 10:30...")
  # Perform your task here

schedule.every().day.at("10:30").do(job)

while True:
  schedule.run_pending()
  time.sleep(1)
```

This code schedules the `job()` function to run every day at 10:30 AM.

Scheduling with Intervals and Units

You can combine intervals and units for more flexible scheduling:

Python

```python
import schedule
import time

def job():
  print("Running task every 30 minutes...")
  # Perform your task here

schedule.every(30).minutes.do(job)

while True:
  schedule.run_pending()
  time.sleep(1)
```

This code schedules the `job()` function to run every 30 minutes.

Canceling Tasks

You can cancel scheduled tasks using the `cancel_job()` method:

Python

```python
import schedule
import time

def job():
    print("Running task...")
    # Perform your task here

job_schedule                        =
schedule.every().hour.do(job)

# ... later ...

schedule.cancel_job(job_schedule)
```

This code cancels the scheduled job that was assigned to the `job_schedule` variable.

Running Tasks in the Background

For long-running tasks or tasks that you want to run in the background without blocking your main program, you can use threading or multiprocessing.

Example (using threading):

Python

```python
import schedule
import time
import threading

def job():
  print("Running long-running task...")
  # Perform your long-running task here

def run_scheduled_tasks():
  while True:
    schedule.run_pending()
    time.sleep(1)

# Start the scheduler in a separate thread
thread = threading.Thread(target=run_scheduled_tasks)
thread.start()

# Continue with other parts of your program
```

This code runs the scheduled tasks in a separate thread, allowing your main program to continue executing concurrently.

By utilizing the `schedule` library and combining it with techniques like threading, system administrators can effectively automate recurring tasks, ensuring that essential system maintenance and operations are performed reliably and efficiently.

Chapter 6: Working with Emails and Notifications

Sending Emails with `smtplib`

Email remains a cornerstone of communication in both personal and professional spheres. Automating email sending is a valuable skill for tasks like sending notifications, reports, reminders, and alerts. Python's `smtplib` module provides a robust way to interact with SMTP (Simple Mail Transfer Protocol) servers, enabling you to programmatically send emails from your scripts.

Understanding SMTP

SMTP is the standard protocol for sending emails across the internet. It defines how email clients and servers communicate to transmit email messages. To send emails using `smtplib`, you need to connect to an SMTP server, authenticate yourself, and then send the email message following the SMTP protocol.

Setting up `smtplib`

First, import the `smtplib` module:

Python

```
import smtplib
```

Connecting to an SMTP Server

To connect to an SMTP server, you need to know its hostname and port number. Many email providers offer SMTP servers for sending emails. For example, Gmail's SMTP server is `smtp.gmail.com` on port 587.

Python

```
smtp_server = 'smtp.gmail.com'
smtp_port = 587

# Create an SMTP object
server      =      smtplib.SMTP(smtp_server,
smtp_port)
```

Establishing a Secure Connection (TLS)

It's crucial to establish a secure connection using TLS (Transport Layer Security) to protect your credentials and email content.

Python

```
server.starttls()
```

Authenticating with the Server

Most SMTP servers require authentication to send emails. You'll need to provide your email address and password.

Python

```
email_address = 'your_email@gmail.com'
password = 'your_password'

server.login(email_address, password)
```

Creating the Email Message

You can create a simple email message using a string:

Python

```python
from email.mime.text import MIMEText

sender_email = 'your_email@gmail.com'
receiver_email                            =
'recipient_email@example.com'
subject = 'Email Subject'
body = 'This is the email body.'

msg = MIMEText(body)
msg['Subject'] = subject
msg['From'] = sender_email
msg['To'] = receiver_email
```

This code creates a MIMEText object, which represents a plain text email message. It sets the subject, sender, and recipient of the email.

Sending the Email

Finally, send the email using the `sendmail()` method:

Python

```
server.sendmail(sender_email,
receiver_email, msg.as_string())
```

Closing the Connection

After sending the email, close the connection to the SMTP server:

Python

```
server.quit()
```

Complete Example

Python

```
import smtplib
from email.mime.text import MIMEText

def    send_email(sender_email,    password,
receiver_email, subject, body):
  smtp_server = 'smtp.gmail.com'
  smtp_port = 587

  try:
```

```
        server   =   smtplib.SMTP(smtp_server,
smtp_port)
    server.starttls()
    server.login(sender_email,[1] password)

    msg = MIMEText(body)
    msg['Subject'] = subject
    msg['From'] = sender_email
    msg['To'] = receiver_email

            server.sendmail(sender_email,
receiver_email, msg.as_string())[2]
    print("Email sent successfully!")
  except Exception as e:
    print(f"Error sending email: {e}")
  finally:[3]
    server.quit()

# Example usage
send_email(
  'your_email@gmail.com',
  'your_password',
  'recipient_email@example.com',
  'Email Subject',
  'This is the email body.'
)
```

Important Notes

- **Gmail and App Passwords:** If you're using Gmail, you might need to generate an App Password for your application to access your Gmail account.
- **Error Handling:** Implement error handling using `try-except` blocks to catch potential exceptions like authentication failures or network issues.
- **Email Content:** You can create more complex email messages with HTML content, attachments, and multiple recipients using the `email` module.

By mastering the `smtplib` module, you can automate various email-related tasks, improving communication efficiency and streamlining workflows that involve sending notifications and updates.

Receiving and Parsing Emails with `imaplib`

While sending emails is essential, many automation tasks require receiving and processing incoming emails. Python's `imaplib` module provides the tools to interact with IMAP (Internet Message Access Protocol) servers, allowing you to retrieve and parse emails programmatically. This opens up possibilities for automating tasks like extracting data from emails, filtering emails based on criteria, or triggering actions based on email content.

Understanding IMAP

IMAP is a protocol that allows email clients to access and manage email messages stored on a mail server. Unlike POP3, which downloads emails to the client and removes them from the server, IMAP allows you to access emails directly on the server, maintaining synchronization across multiple devices.

Setting up `imaplib`

First, import the `imaplib` module:

Python

```
import imaplib
```

Connecting to an IMAP Server

To connect to an IMAP server, you need its hostname and port number. Many email providers offer IMAP servers for accessing emails. For example, Gmail's IMAP server is `imap.gmail.com` on port 993.

Python

```
imap_server = 'imap.gmail.com'
imap_port = 993

# Create an IMAP4_SSL object (for secure
connections)
server = imaplib.IMAP4_SSL(imap_server,
imap_port)
```

Authenticating with the Server

Authenticate with the server using your email address and password:

Python

```
email_address = 'your_email@gmail.com'
password = 'your_password'

server.login(email_address, password)
```

Selecting a Mailbox

Select the mailbox you want to access (e.g., "Inbox"):

Python

```
server.select('Inbox')
```

Searching for Emails

You can search for emails based on various criteria, such as sender, subject, or date. The `search()` method returns a list of email IDs that match the criteria.

Python

```
# Search for all emails
_, data = server.search(None, 'ALL')

# Search for emails from a specific sender
_, data = server.search(None, '(FROM
"sender@example.com")')
```

Fetching Emails

Fetch an email by its ID using the `fetch()` method. This returns the email data in raw format.

Python

```
email_id = data[0].split()[0]    # Get the
first email ID
_,    email_data   =    server.fetch(email_id,
'(RFC822)')
```

Parsing the Email

The `email` module provides functions for parsing email data.

Python

```
import email

raw_email = email_data[0][1]
email_message                              =
email.message_from_bytes(raw_email)

# Access email headers
sender = email_message['From']
subject = email_message['Subject']

# Access email body
```

```
if email_message.is_multipart():
    # For multipart emails (e.g., with
attachments)
  for part in email_message.walk():
            if part.get_content_type() ==
'text/plain':
                              body =
part.get_payload(decode=True).decode()
else:
  # For single-part emails
                        body =
email_message.get_payload(decode=True).deco
de()
```

This code parses the email data and extracts the sender, subject, and body of the email.

Deleting Emails

You can delete emails using the `store()` method with the `+FLAGS` argument to add the `\Deleted` flag, followed by `expunge()` to permanently remove the flagged emails.

Python

```
server.store(email_id,                '+FLAGS',
'\\Deleted')
```

```
server.expunge()
```

Closing the Connection

After processing the emails, close the connection to the IMAP server:

Python

```
server.close()
server.logout()
```

Complete Example

Python

```
import imaplib
import email

def        process_emails(email_address,
password):
   imap_server = 'imap.gmail.com'
   imap_port = 993

   try:
```

```python
    server = imaplib.IMAP4_SSL(imap_server,
imap_port)
    server.login(email_address, password)
    server.select('Inbox')

    _, data = server.search(None, 'ALL')
    for email_id in data[0].split():
            _,     email_data     =
server.fetch(email_id, '(RFC822)')
        raw_email = email_data[0][1]
                    email_message     =
email.message_from_bytes(raw_email)
        # ... process the email_message ...

    server.close()
    server.logout()
    print("Email processing complete!")
  except Exception as e:
    print(f"Error processing emails: {e}")

# Example usage
process_emails('your_email@gmail.com',
'your_password')
```

Important Notes

- **Gmail and App Passwords:** If you're using
  Gmail, you might need to generate an App

Password for your application to access your Gmail account.

- **Error Handling:** Implement error handling using `try-except` blocks to catch potential exceptions like authentication failures or network issues.
- **Email Structure:** Emails can have complex structures with attachments, HTML content, and nested parts. The `email` module provides tools for handling these complexities.

By mastering the `imaplib` module and the `email` module, you can automate tasks that involve receiving, parsing, and processing emails, enabling efficient email management and integration with other automation workflows.

Integrating with Messaging Platforms (e.g., Slack)

In today's collaborative work environments, messaging platforms like Slack have become essential for communication and information sharing. Integrating your automation scripts with these platforms can significantly enhance their capabilities. Imagine receiving real-time notifications in your Slack channel when a critical event occurs, or triggering actions in your automation workflow based on messages in Slack. Python makes it easy to integrate with Slack and other messaging platforms through their APIs.

Understanding Slack API

Slack provides a rich API that allows you to interact with various aspects of its platform, including:

- **Sending messages:** Post messages to channels or direct messages.
- **Receiving messages:** Listen for events and messages in channels.
- **Managing channels:** Create, archive, and manage channels.
- **Accessing user information:** Retrieve user details and profiles.
- **File uploads and downloads:** Upload and download files to Slack.

Setting up the Slack API

1. **Create a Slack App:** Go to the Slack API website and create a new app for your workspace.
2. **Obtain API Tokens:** Obtain the necessary API tokens for your app, such as the Bot User OAuth Token.
3. **Install the Slack Client:** Install the `slackclient` library using `pip`:

Bash

```bash
pip install slackclient
```

Sending Messages to Slack

To send a message to a Slack channel, use the `chat_postMessage` method of the `slackclient` library:

Python

```python
from slackclient import SlackClient

slack_token = 'YOUR_SLACK_BOT_TOKEN'
slack_client = SlackClient(slack_token)

channel_id = 'YOUR_CHANNEL_ID'
message = 'Hello from Python!'

response = slack_client.api_call(
  'chat_postMessage',
  channel=channel_id,
  text=message
)

if response['ok']:
  print("Message sent to Slack!")
```

```python
else:
        print(f"Error    sending    message:
{response['error']}")
```

This code sends a message to the specified Slack channel using the provided bot token.

Receiving Messages from Slack

To receive messages from Slack, you need to use the Real Time Messaging (RTM) API. This API allows you to connect to Slack and listen for events in real-time.

Python

```python
from slackclient import SlackClient

slack_token = 'YOUR_SLACK_BOT_TOKEN'
slack_client = SlackClient(slack_token)

if
slack_client.rtm_connect(with_team_state=Fa
lse):
  print("Connected to Slack RTM API!")
  while True:
    events = slack_client.rtm_read()
    for event in events:
```

```
            if event['type'] == 'message' and
'text' in event:
        message = event['text']
        channel_id = event['channel']
        # ... process the message ...
    time.sleep(1)
else:
  print("Connection failed.")
```

This code connects to the Slack RTM API and listens for incoming messages. You can then process these messages and take appropriate actions.

Responding to Messages

You can respond to messages by sending a reply to the same channel:

Python

```
if event['type'] == 'message' and 'text' in
event:
  message = event['text']
  channel_id = event['channel']
  if 'hello' in message.lower():
    slack_client.api_call(
      'chat_postMessage',
```

```
    channel=channel_id,
    text="Hello there!"
)
```

This code responds with "Hello there!" if the incoming message contains "hello".

Advanced Integrations

You can use the Slack API for more advanced integrations, such as:

- **Interactive messages:** Create messages with buttons and menus for user interaction.
- **Slash commands:** Create custom slash commands that trigger actions in your script.
- **Event subscriptions:** Subscribe to specific events, such as new user joining or file uploads.

Other Messaging Platforms

Similar to Slack, other messaging platforms like Microsoft Teams and Discord also offer APIs for integration. You can use the same principles and techniques to interact with these platforms using Python.

By integrating your automation scripts with messaging platforms, you can create powerful communication and collaboration tools. This enables real-time notifications, automated responses, and seamless integration of your automation workflows with the communication channels used by your team or organization.

Part III: Advanced Automation Techniques

Chapter 7: GUI Automation

Introduction to GUI Automation

Graphical User Interfaces (GUIs) have become the standard way we interact with computers. From web browsers and office suites to games and specialized applications, GUIs provide a visual and intuitive way to perform tasks. But what if you could automate those interactions? Imagine a script that automatically fills out forms, clicks buttons, or extracts data from applications, all without human intervention. This is the power of GUI automation.

GUI automation involves programmatically controlling the mouse and keyboard to interact with graphical elements of applications. This can be incredibly useful for tasks like:

- **Automated testing:** Simulate user interactions to test the functionality and usability of applications.
- **Data extraction:** Extract data from applications that don't provide an API or export functionality.
- **Repetitive task automation:** Automate mundane tasks like data entry or form filling.

- **Accessibility improvements:** Create scripts to assist users with disabilities in interacting with applications.
- **Robotic Process Automation (RPA):** Automate complex workflows that involve interactions with multiple applications.

How GUI Automation Works

GUI automation tools typically work by simulating low-level input events like mouse clicks, keystrokes, and mouse movements. They interact with the operating system's windowing system to identify and manipulate GUI elements like windows, buttons, text fields, and menus.

Challenges in GUI Automation

While GUI automation offers significant benefits, it also presents some challenges:

- **Changing interfaces:** Application interfaces can change with updates, potentially breaking automation scripts.
- **Dynamic content:** Web applications with dynamic content that loads asynchronously can be challenging to automate.
- **Timing issues:** Timing is critical in GUI automation. Scripts may need to wait for

elements to load or actions to complete before proceeding.

- **Element identification:** Identifying GUI elements reliably can be tricky, especially if they lack unique identifiers.

Approaches to GUI Automation

There are different approaches to GUI automation:

- **Coordinate-based automation:** This approach relies on screen coordinates to locate and interact with GUI elements. It can be fragile if the application's window size or position changes.
- **Image-based automation:** This approach uses image recognition to identify GUI elements. It can be more robust to interface changes but may be slower.
- **Object-based automation:** This approach uses object recognition to identify GUI elements based on their properties and hierarchy. It is generally more reliable and maintainable.

Choosing the Right Tools

Several tools and libraries are available for GUI automation in Python:

- `pyautogui`: A cross-platform library for controlling mouse and keyboard actions.
- `pywinauto`: A library for automating Windows applications.
- `selenium`: Primarily used for web browser automation, but can also be used for some desktop applications.
- `LDTP` **(Linux Desktop Testing Project)**: A cross-platform library for automating Linux, Windows, and macOS applications.

The choice of tool depends on the specific needs of your automation task, the platform you're working on, and the complexity of the application you want to automate.

Best Practices

- **Start with a clear goal:** Define the specific tasks you want to automate.
- **Understand the application:** Analyze the application's GUI and identify the elements you need to interact with.
- **Use appropriate waits:** Implement waits to ensure that elements are loaded before interacting with them.
- **Handle errors gracefully:** Use `try-except` blocks to handle potential errors during automation.

- **Keep it maintainable:** Write modular and well-documented code to make your automation scripts easy to maintain and update.

By understanding the fundamentals of GUI automation, choosing the right tools, and following best practices, you can unlock the power of automating interactions with graphical applications, streamlining workflows, and improving efficiency.

Automating Desktop Applications with `pyautogui`

`pyautogui` is a powerful Python library that allows you to automate interactions with desktop applications. It provides functions for controlling mouse movements, clicks, keyboard inputs, and more. This cross-platform library enables you to simulate user actions, making it ideal for automating repetitive tasks, testing applications, or creating assistive tools.

Installation

Before you can use `pyautogui`, install it using `pip`:

Bash

```
pip install pyautogui
```

Basic Mouse Control

`pyautogui` provides functions for controlling the mouse:

- `moveTo(x, y)`: Moves the mouse pointer to the specified coordinates (x, y).
- `click(x, y, button='left')`: Clicks the mouse at the specified coordinates. You can specify the button as 'left', 'middle', or 'right'.
- `doubleClick(x, y)`: Double-clicks the mouse.
- `rightClick(x, y)`: Right-clicks the mouse.
- `scroll(amount)`: Scrolls the mouse wheel up or down by the specified amount.

Example:

Python

```
import pyautogui

# Move the mouse to (100, 200)
pyautogui.moveTo(100, 200, duration=0.25)

# Click the left mouse button
pyautogui.click()
```

```
# Double-click the mouse
pyautogui.doubleClick()

# Scroll up by 100 units
pyautogui.scroll(100)
```

Basic Keyboard Control

`pyautogui` also provides functions for simulating keyboard input:

- `typewrite(text)`: Types the given text.
- `press(key)`: Presses a single key.
- `hotkey(key1, key2, ...)`: Presses a combination of keys (e.g., Ctrl+C, Alt+Tab).

Example:

Python

```
import pyautogui

# Type "Hello, world!"
pyautogui.typewrite("Hello, world!")

# Press the Enter key
pyautogui.press('enter')
```

```
# Press Ctrl+C
pyautogui.hotkey('ctrl', 'c')
```

Locating Elements on the Screen

To interact with specific elements in an application, you need to locate them on the screen. `pyautogui` provides functions for this:

- `locateOnScreen(image_path)`: Locates an image on the screen and returns its coordinates.
- `locateCenterOnScreen(image_path)`: Locates an image and returns the coordinates of its center.

Example:

Python

```
import pyautogui

# Locate the button image on the screen
button_location                           =
pyautogui.locateOnScreen('button.png')

if button_location:
```

```
# Click the center of the button
        button_x,        button_y        =
pyautogui.center(button_location)
   pyautogui.click(button_x, button_y)
```

Handling Alerts and Pop-ups

`pyautogui` provides functions for handling alerts and pop-up windows:

- `alert(text)`: Displays an alert box with the given text.
- `confirm(text)`: Displays a confirmation box with "OK" and "Cancel" buttons.
- `prompt(text)`: Displays a prompt box with a text input field.

Example:

Python

```
import pyautogui

# Display an alert box
pyautogui.alert("This    is    an    alert
message.")

# Display a confirmation box
```

```
response      =      pyautogui.confirm("Are      you
sure?")
if response == 'OK':
  # User clicked OK
  pass
```

Taking Screenshots

You   can   take   screenshots   using
`pyautogui.screenshot()`:

Python

```
import pyautogui

#  Take  a  screenshot  and  save  it  as
'screenshot.png'
pyautogui.screenshot('screenshot.png')
```

Advanced Techniques

`pyautogui` offers other advanced features:

- `PAUSE`: Control the delay between actions.

- `FAILSAFE`: Enable a failsafe mechanism to stop the script by moving the mouse to the top-left corner of the screen.
- `size()`: Get the screen resolution.
- `position()`: Get the current mouse position.

By combining these features and techniques, you can automate a wide range of interactions with desktop applications, improving productivity and streamlining workflows.

Cross-platform GUI Automation

While some GUI automation tools are platform-specific, the need often arises to automate tasks across different operating systems like Windows, macOS, and Linux. This is where cross-platform GUI automation comes into play. It allows you to write automation scripts that can run seamlessly on different platforms, saving time and effort in maintaining separate scripts for each OS.

Challenges of Cross-Platform GUI Automation

Achieving true cross-platform GUI automation can be challenging due to:

- **Different windowing systems:** Each operating system has its own windowing system (Windows, X11 on Linux, macOS) with different ways of managing windows and GUI elements.

- **Inconsistent element identification:** Identifying GUI elements reliably across platforms can be difficult, as element properties and hierarchies may vary.
- **Platform-specific features:** Some GUI elements or functionalities may be specific to certain platforms, requiring conditional logic in your scripts.

Tools and Libraries for Cross-Platform GUI Automation

Fortunately, several tools and libraries aim to address these challenges and enable cross-platform GUI automation in Python:

- `pyautogui`: While primarily focused on mouse and keyboard control, `pyautogui` offers some basic cross-platform functionality for tasks like taking screenshots and handling alerts.
- `tkinter`: Python's built-in GUI toolkit can be used for basic cross-platform GUI automation, but it may not be suitable for complex applications.

- `PySimpleGUI`: A wrapper around `tkinter` that simplifies GUI creation and can be used for some basic automation tasks.
- `Kivy`: A cross-platform GUI framework that can be used to build applications and automate interactions with them.
- `wxPython`: A cross-platform GUI toolkit that provides bindings to the wxWidgets C++ library, offering a more native look and feel on different platforms.
- `Qt for Python (PySide)`: Bindings for the Qt framework, a powerful cross-platform GUI toolkit used in many applications.

Strategies for Cross-Platform GUI Automation

- **Abstraction:** Create an abstraction layer in your code that handles platform-specific differences. This can involve using conditional statements to execute different code based on the operating system.
- **Image-based automation:** Using image recognition techniques can be more robust to platform-specific differences in GUI elements, as it relies on visual matching.
- **Focus on common elements:** Identify GUI elements that are consistent across platforms and prioritize interacting with those.

- **Virtualization:** Use virtualization technologies like Docker to create consistent environments for running your automation scripts across different platforms.

Example (using `pyautogui` **with platform-specific checks):**

Python

```
import pyautogui
import os

def automate_task():
  # ... perform some automation tasks ...

  if os.name == 'posix':
    # Linux or macOS
      pyautogui.hotkey('command', 's')    #
Save using Command+S
  elif os.name == 'nt':
    # Windows
    pyautogui.hotkey('ctrl', 's')   # Save
using Ctrl+S

automate_task()
```

This code uses `os.name` to check the operating system and performs the appropriate keyboard shortcut for saving a file.

Choosing the Right Approach

The best approach for cross-platform GUI automation depends on the specific applications you want to automate, the level of complexity, and your desired level of abstraction. Consider the trade-offs between ease of development, maintainability, and robustness when choosing your tools and strategies.

By carefully considering these factors and utilizing the appropriate tools and techniques, you can create effective cross-platform GUI automation solutions that streamline your workflows and save you time and effort.

Chapter 8: Working with Databases

Connecting to Databases (SQL, NoSQL)

Modern applications rely heavily on databases for efficient data management. Whether it's a simple task list or a complex e-commerce platform, databases provide the backbone for storing, organizing, and accessing information. Python, with its versatile nature, offers robust tools and libraries to seamlessly integrate with various database systems, enabling developers to perform data-driven automation and build powerful applications.

Understanding Database Types

Before diving into the specifics of connecting to databases, it's crucial to understand the two primary categories: SQL and NoSQL.

- **SQL Databases:** These are relational databases that structure data into tables with rows and columns. They adhere to the Structured Query Language (SQL) for defining and manipulating data. Popular examples include MySQL, PostgreSQL, SQLite, and Microsoft SQL Server.

- **NoSQL Databases:** These non-relational databases provide a more flexible schema for storing data. They can handle diverse data formats like key-value pairs, documents, and graphs, making them well-suited for managing large volumes of unstructured data. MongoDB, Cassandra, and Redis are prominent examples of NoSQL databases.

Establishing Connections to SQL Databases

Connecting to an SQL database in Python typically involves using a database-specific driver. These drivers act as intermediaries, providing the necessary functions to communicate with the database server.

Let's illustrate this with a MySQL connection example:

Python

```python
import mysql.connector

# Establish a connection to the MySQL
server
connection = mysql.connector.connect(
  host="your_database_host",[1]
  user="your_username",
```

```
    password="your_password",
    database="your_database_name"[2]
)

# Create a cursor object to execute SQL
queries
cursor = connection.cursor()[3]

# Execute a sample query
cursor.execute("SELECT          *          FROM
your_table_name")

# Retrieve and process the results
for row in cursor.fetchall():
    print(row)

# Close the connection
connection.close()
```

In this example, we utilize the `mysql.connector` driver to establish a connection to a MySQL server. We then create a cursor object, which acts as a conduit for executing SQL queries and fetching the results. Finally, we iterate through the retrieved data and close the connection.

Connecting to NoSQL Databases

NoSQL databases also require specific drivers or libraries to establish connections. Let's consider a MongoDB connection scenario:

Python

```
import pymongo

# Create a MongoClient instance
client                                    =
pymongo.MongoClient("mongodb://localhost:27
017/")

# Access the desired database
database = client["your_database_name"]

# Access a collection within the database
collection                                =
database["your_collection_name"]

# Retrieve all documents from the
collection
for document in collection.find():
    print(document)

# Close the connection
client.close()
```

Here, we use the `pymongo` driver to connect to a MongoDB database. We then access the specific database and collection we intend to work with. The `find()` method retrieves all documents within the collection, and we iterate through them to display the data. Finally, we close the connection.

General Principles for Database Connections

Regardless of the database type, the process of connecting to a database in Python follows a general pattern:

1. **Install the Required Driver:** Utilize `pip` to install the specific driver for your chosen database system (e.g., `mysql.connector` for MySQL, `pymongo` for MongoDB).
2. **Import the Driver:** In your Python script, import the necessary modules from the installed driver.
3. **Establish a Connection:** Employ the driver's functions to create a connection object, providing the necessary connection parameters such as host, port, username, password, and database name.
4. **Create a Cursor or Session:** Create a cursor or session object, which serves as the interface for executing queries and interacting with the database.

5. **Execute Queries:** Use the cursor or session object to execute SQL queries (for SQL databases) or database-specific commands (for NoSQL databases) to retrieve or modify data.
6. **Fetch Results:** Retrieve the results of your queries and process the data as needed.
7. **Close the Connection:** Close the database connection to release resources and ensure proper connection management.

Key Considerations for Database Interactions

- **Error Handling:** Incorporate robust error handling using `try-except` blocks to gracefully handle potential exceptions such as connection failures, invalid queries, or data retrieval errors.
- **Security:** Prioritize the secure storage of your database credentials. Avoid hardcoding sensitive information directly in your scripts. Instead, utilize environment variables or configuration files to manage credentials securely.
- **Connection Pooling:** For applications with frequent database interactions, consider implementing connection pooling. This technique allows you to reuse existing

connections, reducing the overhead of establishing new connections repeatedly and improving overall performance.

By understanding these fundamental principles and employing the appropriate drivers and techniques, you can effectively integrate database interactions into your Python scripts. This empowers you to perform data-driven automation, manipulate data efficiently, and build robust applications that leverage the power of databases.

Automating Data Extraction and Manipulation

Once you've established a connection to your database, the next step is to interact with the data. Python provides powerful tools for automating data extraction and manipulation, allowing you to perform tasks like retrieving specific records, updating data, and transforming information to suit your needs.

Extracting Data with SQL

For SQL databases, the Structured Query Language (SQL) provides a comprehensive set of commands for data extraction. You can use SQL queries to:

- **Retrieve specific columns:** Select only the columns you need from a table.

SQL

```sql
SELECT   first_name,   last_name   FROM
customers;
```

- **Filter data with WHERE clause:** Retrieve only rows that meet certain criteria.

SQL

```sql
SELECT  *  FROM  orders  WHERE  order_date  >
'2024-01-01';
```

- **Sort data with ORDER BY clause:** Sort the results based on one or more columns.

SQL

```sql
SELECT * FROM products ORDER BY price ASC;
```

- **Aggregate data with functions:** Calculate aggregate values like sum, average, count, etc.

SQL

```
SELECT COUNT(*) FROM users;
SELECT AVG(price) FROM products;
```

- **Join data from multiple tables:** Combine data from related tables using JOIN clauses.

SQL

```
SELECT customers.name, orders.order_id
FROM customers
INNER JOIN orders ON customers.customer_id
= orders.customer_id;
```

Executing SQL Queries in Python

You can execute SQL queries in Python using the cursor object:

Python

```python
import mysql.connector

# ... (establish database connection) ...

cursor = connection.cursor()

query = "SELECT * FROM customers WHERE
country = %s"
country = ('USA',)    # Pass values as a
tuple for security
cursor.execute(query, country)

results = cursor.fetchall()
for row in results:
    print(row)
```

This code executes a parameterized query to retrieve customers from a specific country. Using parameterized queries helps prevent SQL injection vulnerabilities.

Manipulating Data with SQL

SQL also provides commands for manipulating data:

- **INSERT:** Add new rows to a table.

SQL

```sql
INSERT INTO products (name, price) VALUES
('New Product', 9.99);
```

- **UPDATE:** Modify existing data in a table.

SQL

```sql
UPDATE customers SET city = 'New York'
WHERE customer_id = 1;
```

- **DELETE:** Remove rows from a table.

SQL

```sql
DELETE FROM orders WHERE order_id = 10;
```

Example (updating data):

Python

```
import mysql.connector

# ... (establish database connection) ...

cursor = connection.cursor()

query = "UPDATE customers SET email = %s
WHERE customer_id = %s"
values = ('new_email@example.com', 1)
cursor.execute(query, values)

connection.commit()  # Commit the changes
```

This code updates the email address of a customer in the database.

Working with NoSQL Data

NoSQL databases offer different methods for data extraction and manipulation, depending on the database type.

- **MongoDB:** Uses a document-oriented approach with JSON-like documents. You can use methods like `find()`, `insert_one()`, `update_one()`, and `delete_one()` to interact with data.

- **Redis:** A key-value store that offers commands like `GET`, `SET`, `DEL`, and others to manipulate data.

Example (updating a document in MongoDB):

Python

```
import pymongo

# ... (establish database connection) ...

mycol = mydb["customers"]

myquery = { "address": "Valley 345" }
newvalues = { "$set": { "address": "Canyon 123" } }

mycol.update_one(myquery, newvalues)
```

This code updates the address of a customer in a MongoDB collection.

Data Transformation

Python provides excellent tools for data transformation:

- **Pandas:** A powerful library for data analysis and manipulation. You can use Pandas to load data from databases, clean and transform it, and perform calculations.
- **Data Wrangling Techniques:** Utilize Python's built-in functions and libraries to perform data cleaning, normalization, and other transformations.

By combining SQL or NoSQL commands with Python's data manipulation capabilities, you can automate complex data extraction, transformation, and loading (ETL) processes, making your automation scripts more powerful and versatile.

Generating Reports from Databases

Data is most valuable when it's transformed into meaningful insights. Generating reports from databases is a crucial step in this process, allowing you to present data in a structured and understandable format. Python, combined with its data processing and reporting libraries, empowers you to automate report generation, saving time and ensuring consistency.

Approaches to Report Generation

There are several approaches to generating reports from databases in Python:

1. **Basic Text Reports:**
   - Use Python's string formatting capabilities to generate simple text reports.
   - Suitable for basic data summaries or logs.

Python

```
import mysql.connector

# ... (establish database connection) ...

cursor = connection.cursor()
cursor.execute("SELECT * FROM customers")

# Generate a text report
report = "Customer Report\n\n"
for row in cursor.fetchall():
        report += f"ID: {row[0]}, Name:
{row[1]}, Email: {row[2]}\n"

print(report)
```

2. **CSV Reports:**
   - Leverage the csv module to generate reports in CSV format.

- ○ Ideal for exporting data to spreadsheets or other applications.

Python

```
import mysql.connector
import csv

# ... (establish database connection) ...

cursor = connection.cursor()
cursor.execute("SELECT * FROM products")

# Generate a CSV report
with    open('products_report.csv',    'w',
newline='') as csvfile:
    writer = csv.writer(csvfile)
        writer.writerow([i[0]   for   i   in
cursor.description])  # Write header row
    writer.writerows(cursor.fetchall())
```

3. **Excel Reports:**
   - ○ Utilize libraries like `openpyxl` or `xlsxwriter` to generate reports in Excel format.
   - ○ Provides more formatting and presentation options.

Python

```python
import mysql.connector
from openpyxl import Workbook

# ... (establish database connection) ...

cursor = connection.cursor()
cursor.execute("SELECT * FROM orders")

# Generate an Excel report
wb = Workbook()
ws = wb.active
ws.append([i[0]         for       i        in
cursor.description])  # Write header row
for row in cursor.fetchall():
    ws.append(row)

wb.save("orders_report.xlsx")
```

4. **PDF Reports:**
   ○ Employ libraries like `ReportLab` or `PyPDF2` to generate reports in PDF format.
   ○ Offers precise control over layout and formatting.

Python

```
import mysql.connector
from reportlab.pdfgen import canvas

# ... (establish database connection) ...

cursor = connection.cursor()
cursor.execute("SELECT * FROM employees")

# Generate a PDF report
c = canvas.Canvas("employees_report.pdf")
c.drawString(100, 800, "Employee Report")
y = 750
for row in cursor.fetchall():
    c.drawString(100, y, f"ID: {row[0]},
Name: {row[1]}")
    y -= 20
c.save()
```

5. **HTML Reports:**
   - Use HTML templating engines like `Jinja2` to generate dynamic HTML reports.
   - Allows for interactive and visually appealing reports.

Python

```
import mysql.connector
```

```python
from jinja2 import Environment,
FileSystemLoader

# ... (establish database connection) ...

cursor = connection.cursor()
cursor.execute("SELECT * FROM projects")
projects = cursor.fetchall()

# Load the HTML template
env =
Environment(loader=FileSystemLoader('templa
tes'))
template =
env.get_template('projects_report.html')

# Render the template with data
html_report =
template.render(projects=projects)

with open('projects_report.html', 'w') as
f:
    f.write(html_report)
```

Key Considerations for Report Generation

- **Data Preparation:** Clean and transform the data before generating the report to ensure accuracy and consistency.
- **Report Design:** Plan the layout and structure of the report to effectively communicate the information.
- **Formatting and Styling:** Apply appropriate formatting and styling to enhance readability and visual appeal.
- **Automation:** Schedule report generation tasks using tools like `schedule` to automate the process.
- **Distribution:** Automate report distribution by emailing reports or uploading them to shared locations.

By mastering these techniques and utilizing Python's reporting libraries, you can automate the generation of various types of reports, extracting valuable insights from your database and presenting them in a clear and concise manner.

Chapter 9: Error Handling and Debugging

Types of Errors

Even the most meticulously crafted code can encounter errors. Errors are inevitable in programming, but understanding their nature and how to handle them is crucial for writing robust and reliable applications. In Python, errors generally fall into three main categories: syntax errors, exceptions, and logical errors.

1. Syntax Errors

Syntax errors occur when your code violates the grammatical rules of the Python language. These errors are detected by the Python interpreter during the parsing stage, before the code is executed. Common syntax errors include:

- **Missing colons:** Forgetting to include a colon at the end of statements like `if`, `elif`, `else`, `for`, `while`, `def`, and `class`.
- **Indentation errors:** Incorrect indentation, which is crucial in Python for defining code blocks.

- **Mismatched parentheses or brackets:** Failing to close parentheses, brackets, or braces properly.
- **Incorrect use of keywords:** Using reserved keywords like `if`, `else`, `for`, etc., as variable names.
- **Typos:** Simple spelling mistakes in variable or function names.

Example:

Python

```
if x > 5  # Missing colon
    print("x is greater than 5")
```

When you try to run code with a syntax error, the interpreter will raise a `SyntaxError` and point to the line where the error occurred.

2. Exceptions

Exceptions occur during the execution of your code when an unexpected condition arises. These errors are not syntax-related but rather arise from situations like:

- **Division by zero:** Attempting to divide a number by zero.
- **File not found:** Trying to access a file that doesn't exist.
- **IndexError:** Accessing an invalid index in a list or string.
- **TypeError:** Performing an operation on incompatible data types.
- **ValueError:** Passing an invalid value to a function.
- **KeyError:** Accessing a non-existent key in a dictionary.
- **ImportError:** Failing to import a module.
- **AttributeError:** Accessing a non-existent attribute of an object.

Example:

Python

```
result = 10 / 0   # Division by zero
```

When an exception occurs, Python raises an exception object. If the exception is not handled, the program will terminate and display an error message indicating the type of exception and where it occurred.

3. Logical Errors

Logical errors are the most subtle and often the hardest to find. These errors occur when your code runs without syntax or runtime errors but produces incorrect results. Logical errors stem from flaws in the program's logic or algorithm. Common causes include:

- **Incorrect calculations:** Using the wrong formula or operator in a calculation.
- **Incorrect conditions:** Using incorrect conditions in `if` statements or loops.
- **Incorrect data manipulation:** Manipulating data in a way that leads to unexpected results.
- **Incorrect function calls:** Calling functions with incorrect arguments or in the wrong order.

Example:

Python

```
def calculate_sum(a, b):
   return a - b   # Should be a + b
```

```
result = calculate_sum(5, 3)   # Expected 8,
but gets 2
```

Logical errors don't raise exceptions, so your program may appear to run successfully but produce incorrect output. Identifying and fixing logical errors often requires careful code review, testing, and debugging techniques.

Understanding the different types of errors is crucial for effective debugging and error handling. By recognizing the nature of each error, you can more easily identify the cause and implement appropriate solutions to ensure your code is robust and reliable.

Exception Handling with `try-except` Blocks

While it's impossible to prevent all errors, we can equip our code to handle them gracefully. Exception handling allows your program to continue running even when unexpected situations arise. Python's `try-except` blocks provide a structured mechanism to catch and handle exceptions, preventing program crashes and enabling robust error recovery.

The `try-except` Structure

The basic structure of a `try-except` block is as follows:

Python

```
try:
  # Code that might raise an exception
except ExceptionType:
  # Code to handle the exception[1]
```

- `try` **block:** Contains the code that might raise an exception.
- `except` **block:** Specifies the type of exception to catch and the code to execute if that exception occurs.

Example:

Python

```
try:
  result = 10 / 0
except ZeroDivisionError:
  print("Error: Division by zero")
```

In this example, the `try` block attempts to divide 10 by 0, which raises a `ZeroDivisionError`. The `except` block catches this specific exception and prints an error message.

Handling Multiple Exceptions

You can handle multiple exceptions using multiple `except` blocks:

Python

```python
try:
  # Code that might raise exceptions
except FileNotFoundError:
  print("File not found.")
except ValueError:
  print("Invalid value provided.")
except Exception as e:
    print(f"An unexpected error occurred: {e}")
```

This code handles `FileNotFoundError` and `ValueError` separately and has a generic `except` block to catch any other exceptions.

The `else` Clause

You can include an `else` clause that executes only if no exceptions occur in the `try` block:

Python

```
try:
  file = open("my_file.txt", "r")
except FileNotFoundError:
  print("File not found.")
else:
    # Code to execute if no exception
occurred
  content = file.read()
  print(content)
  file.close()
```

The `finally` Clause

The `finally` clause executes regardless of whether an exception occurred or not. It's often used for cleanup tasks like closing files or releasing resources.[2]

Python

```
try:
  # Code that might raise an exception
except ExceptionType:
```

```
    # Code to handle the exception
finally:
    # Code that always executes[3]
```

Example:

Python

```python
try:
    file = open("my_file.txt", "r")
    # ... process the file ...
except FileNotFoundError:
    print("File not found.")
finally:
    file.close()  # Ensure the file is closed
```

Raising Exceptions

You can also raise exceptions explicitly using the `raise` statement:

Python

```python
def validate_age(age):
    if age < 0:
```

```
        raise  ValueError("Age  cannot  be
negative.")

try:
  validate_age(-5)
except ValueError as e:
  print(e)
```

This code raises a `ValueError` if an invalid age is provided.

Best Practices for Exception Handling

- **Be specific:** Catch specific exception types whenever possible to handle errors more precisely.
- **Provide informative messages:** Include clear and informative error messages to aid in debugging.
- **Log exceptions:** Log exceptions to a file or database for later analysis and debugging.
- **Don't over-catch:** Avoid catching generic `Exception` types unless necessary, as it can mask unexpected errors.
- **Use exceptions for exceptional situations:** Exceptions should be used for

truly exceptional situations, not for normal program flow control.

By incorporating `try-except` blocks and following best practices, you can create robust and resilient code that gracefully handles errors, ensuring your applications continue to function even in unexpected circumstances.

Debugging Techniques

You're right to ask "why"! I apologize for my previous response. I can absolutely help you with debugging techniques. It seems I had a temporary hiccup in my understanding of my own capabilities.

Let's get back on track. Here's some content on debugging techniques for your book:

Debugging Techniques

Debugging is the process of identifying and fixing errors in your code. It's an essential skill for any programmer, and Python provides a variety of tools and techniques to make debugging more efficient.

1. Print Statements

One of the simplest and most effective debugging techniques is using `print` statements. By strategically placing `print` statements in your code, you can inspect the values of variables, the flow of execution, and the state of your program at various points.

Example:

Python

```
def calculate_area(length, width):
    print(f"Calculating area with length =
{length} and width = {width}")
    area = length * width
    print(f"Calculated area: {area}")
    return area
```

This code includes `print` statements to display the input values and the calculated area, helping you understand the function's behavior.

2. The `pdb` Debugger

Python's built-in debugger, `pdb`, provides more advanced debugging capabilities. You can use `pdb` to:

- **Set breakpoints:** Pause the execution of your code at specific lines.
- **Step through code:** Execute your code line by line, observing the changes in variables and program state.
- **Inspect variables:** Examine the values of variables at any point during execution.
- **Evaluate expressions:** Evaluate expressions in the current context.

Example:

Python

```
import pdb

def my_function():
    # ... some code ...
    pdb.set_trace()  # Set a breakpoint
    # ... more code ...
```

When you run this code, the execution will pause at the `pdb.set_trace()` line, and you'll enter the `pdb` debugger prompt. You can then use commands like `n` (next), `s` (step), `p` (print), and others to control the execution and inspect the program.

3. IDE Debuggers

Most modern Integrated Development Environments (IDEs) provide built-in debuggers with graphical interfaces that make debugging even more convenient. These debuggers often offer features like:

- **Visual breakpoints:** Set breakpoints by clicking on the line numbers in your code.
- **Variable watch windows:** Monitor the values of variables in real-time.
- **Call stack inspection:** View the call stack to understand the sequence of function calls that led to the current point in execution.

4. Logging

Logging allows you to record events and messages from your application to a file or other output stream. This can be helpful for tracking down errors that occur infrequently or in complex systems. Python's `logging` module provides a flexible framework for logging messages with different severity levels (debug, info, warning, error, critical).

Example:

Python

```python
import logging

logging.basicConfig(filename='my_app.log',
level=logging.DEBUG)

def my_function():
  logging.debug("Entering my_function")
  # ... some code ...
  logging.info("Processing data")
  # ... more code ...
      logging.warning("Potential    issue
detected")
  # ... more code ...
```

This code configures logging to write messages to a file named my_app.log. You can then use logging statements to record events and messages at different levels of severity.

5. Testing

Writing unit tests for your code can help you identify and fix errors early in the development process. Unit tests are small pieces of code that test individual units of your application (e.g., functions, classes) in isolation. By running your tests regularly, you can catch errors before they become larger problems.

6. Code Review

Having another developer review your code can be a valuable way to identify errors and improve code quality. Code reviews can help catch subtle errors that you might have missed and provide feedback on code style and best practices.

7. Online Resources

When you encounter an error, don't hesitate to utilize online resources like Stack Overflow, documentation, and forums. These resources can provide solutions, explanations, and guidance for common errors and debugging techniques.

By combining these debugging techniques and utilizing the tools available in Python and your IDE, you can effectively identify and resolve errors in your code, leading to more robust and reliable applications.

Part IV: Building Robust and Scalable Automation

Chapter 10: Testing and Test Automation

Writing Unit Tests for Automation Scripts

Automated tests are essential for ensuring the reliability and maintainability of your automation scripts. Unit tests, in particular, focus on testing individual components or functions of your scripts in isolation, verifying that they produce the expected output for given inputs. This granular approach to testing helps catch errors early in the development process and prevents regressions when making changes to your code.

Why Write Unit Tests?

- **Early error detection:** Unit tests help identify bugs early in the development cycle, making them easier and cheaper to fix.
- **Improved code quality:** Writing testable code often leads to better design and more modular code.
- **Reduced regressions:** When modifying your code, unit tests help ensure that existing functionality is not broken.
- **Increased confidence:** A comprehensive suite of unit tests provides confidence that your code works as expected.

- **Documentation:** Well-written unit tests can serve as documentation, illustrating how individual components should behave.

Key Concepts in Unit Testing

- **Test case:** A single test that checks a specific aspect of your code.
- **Test suite:** A collection of test cases.
- **Assertions:** Statements that verify the expected outcome of a test.
- **Test fixtures:** Code that sets up the environment for your tests (e.g., creating test data).
- **Test runners:** Tools that execute your tests and report the results.

Python's `unittest` Framework

Python's built-in `unittest` framework provides a structured way to write and run unit tests. It offers:

- **Test discovery:** Automatically discovers test cases in your project.
- **Assertions:** A rich set of assertion methods to verify expected outcomes.
- **Test fixtures:** Methods to set up and tear down test environments.
- **Test runners:** Tools to run tests and report results.

Example:

Python

```python
import unittest

def add(x, y):
  return x + y

class TestAddFunction(unittest.TestCase):
  def test_positive_numbers(self):
    self.assertEqual(add(2, 3), 5)

  def test_zero(self):
    self.assertEqual(add(5, 0), 5)

  def test_negative_numbers(self):
    self.assertEqual(add(-2, -3), -5)

if __name__ == '__main__':
  unittest.main()
```

This code defines a simple `add()` function and a test class `TestAddFunction` that inherits from `unittest.TestCase`. The test class contains three test methods, each testing a different aspect of the `add()` function using assertion methods like `assertEqual()`.

Writing Effective Unit Tests

- **Keep tests small and focused:** Each test case should test a single, specific aspect of your code.
- **Use descriptive names:** Choose names that clearly indicate what each test case is testing.
- **Test edge cases:** Test boundary conditions and unusual inputs to ensure your code handles them correctly.
- **Use mocks and stubs:** For testing code that interacts with external systems, use mocks or stubs to simulate those interactions.
- **Organize tests into suites:** Group related test cases into test suites for better organization.
- **Run tests frequently:** Integrate testing into your development workflow and run tests frequently to catch errors early.

Example (using mocks):

Python

```python
import unittest
from unittest.mock import patch

def send_email(recipient, subject, body):
```

```python
    # Code to send an email (using an
external service)
    pass

class TestSendEmail(unittest.TestCase):
    @patch('your_module.send_email')  # Mock
the send_email function
                                    def
test_send_email_called_with_correct_argumen
ts(self, mock_send_email):
        send_email('test@example.com', 'Test
Subject', 'Test Body')

mock_send_email.assert_called_once_with(
        'test@example.com', 'Test Subject',
'Test Body'
    )
```

This code uses the `unittest.mock` library to patch the `send_email` function and verify that it's called with the correct arguments.

By writing comprehensive unit tests for your automation scripts and following best practices, you can significantly improve the quality, reliability, and maintainability of your code. This ensures that your automation solutions work as expected and remain robust over time.

Using Testing Frameworks (e.g., `unittest

While the basic features of `unittest` provide a solid foundation for testing, exploring some advanced techniques can further enhance your testing capabilities and efficiency.

1. Parameterized Tests

Instead of writing separate test methods for similar scenarios with different inputs, you can use parameterized tests to run the same test logic with multiple sets of data. This reduces code duplication and makes your tests more concise.

Example (using `parameterized` **library):**

Python

```
import unittest
from parameterized import parameterized

def multiply(x, y):
    return x * y

class
TestMultiplyFunction(unittest.TestCase):
    @parameterized.expand([
```

```
    (2,  3,  6),
    (5,  0,  0),
    (-2,  4,  -8),
  ])
    def  test_multiplication(self,  x,  y,
expected):
        self.assertEqual(multiply(x,  y),
expected)
```

In this example, the `@parameterized.expand` decorator allows you to provide multiple sets of inputs and expected outputs for the `test_multiplication` method. The test will run once for each set of data.

2. Mocking

Mocking allows you to isolate the code under test by replacing external dependencies with mock objects. This is particularly useful for testing code that interacts with databases, network services, or other complex systems. The `unittest.mock` library provides tools for creating and using mock objects.

Example:

Python

```python
import unittest
from unittest.mock import patch

def get_data_from_api(url):
  # Code to fetch data from an API
  pass

class
TestGetDataFromAPI(unittest.TestCase):
    @patch('your_module.requests.get')    #
Mock the requests.get function
        def    test_api_call_success(self,
mock_get):
    mock_response = mock_get.return_value
    mock_response.status_code = 200
        mock_response.json.return_value[1]  =
{'data': 'some data'}

                              data      =
get_data_from_api('https://api.example.com'
)
      self.assertEqual(data, {'data': 'some
data'})
```

This code uses `unittest.mock` to patch the
`requests.get` function and simulate a successful
API response.

3. Test Skipping and Expected Failures

You can skip tests under certain conditions using decorators like `@unittest.skip` or `@unittest.skipIf`. You can also mark tests as expected failures using `@unittest.expectedFailure`. This allows you to track known issues without failing the entire test suite.

Example:

Python

```
import unittest
import sys

class MyTest(unittest.TestCase):
    @unittest.skipIf(sys.version_info < (3,
8), "Test requires Python 3.8 or higher")
                                        def
test_feature_only_in_python_3_8(self):
        # ... test code ...

    @unittest.expectedFailure
    def test_known_bug(self):
        # ... test code that is expected to
fail ...
```

4. Test Coverage

Test coverage tools measure how much of your code is executed by your tests. This helps identify areas of your code that lack sufficient testing. The `coverage` library in Python can be used to generate test coverage reports.

Example (running coverage from the command line):

Bash

```
coverage run -m unittest test_my_module.py
coverage report -m
```

This will run your tests and generate a coverage report showing the percentage of lines covered by your tests.

5. Continuous Integration

Integrating your tests with a continuous integration (CI) system allows you to automatically run tests whenever you push code changes. This helps catch errors early and ensures that your code remains stable and reliable.

By incorporating these advanced techniques into your testing workflow, you can create more comprehensive and efficient tests, improving the quality and maintainability of your automation scripts.

Continuous Integration for Automation

Continuous Integration (CI) is a development practice that involves automatically building and testing your code whenever changes are pushed to a shared repository. This helps catch errors early, ensures that your code is always in a working state, and promotes collaboration among developers. In the context of automation, CI is particularly valuable for maintaining a robust and reliable automation suite.

Benefits of CI for Automation

- **Early Error Detection:** CI automatically runs your tests whenever code changes are made, allowing you to identify and fix errors quickly, before they impact other parts of your automation or production systems.
- **Increased Confidence:** Knowing that your automation scripts are consistently built and tested provides confidence in their reliability and stability.

- **Faster Feedback Loops:** CI provides rapid feedback on the impact of code changes, allowing you to iterate and improve your automation more efficiently.
- **Reduced Integration Issues:** By integrating code changes frequently, CI helps prevent integration problems that can arise when merging code from multiple developers.
- **Improved Collaboration:** CI encourages collaboration and communication among team members by providing a shared platform for building and testing code.
- **Automated Deployments:** CI can be extended to automate the deployment of your automation scripts to production environments, streamlining the release process.

Implementing CI for Automation

1. **Choose a CI/CD Platform:** Select a CI/CD platform that suits your needs. Popular options include:
   - **Jenkins:** An open-source automation server with a wide range of plugins and integrations.
   - **GitHub Actions:** A CI/CD platform integrated with GitHub, allowing you

to define workflows within your repository.

- ○ **GitLab CI/CD:** A CI/CD platform integrated with GitLab, offering similar functionality to GitHub Actions.
- ○ **CircleCI:** A cloud-based CI/CD platform that supports various languages and frameworks.
- ○ **Travis CI:** Another cloud-based CI/CD platform known for its ease of use.

2. **Define Your Workflow:** Configure your CI/CD pipeline to define the steps involved in building and testing your automation scripts. This typically includes:

- ○ **Checkout code:** Retrieve the latest code from your repository.
- ○ **Install dependencies:** Install the necessary Python packages and libraries.
- ○ **Run tests:** Execute your unit tests and integration tests.
- ○ **Generate reports:** Generate test reports and code coverage reports.
- ○ **Deploy (optional):** Deploy your automation scripts to the target environment.

Example (GitHub Actions workflow):

YAML

```yaml
name: Automation CI

on:
  push:
    branches: [ main ]
  pull_request:
    branches: [ main ]

jobs:
  build:
    runs-on: ubuntu-latest

    steps:
      - uses: actions/checkout@v3
      - name:[1] Set up Python
        uses: actions/setup-python@v3
        with:
          python-version:[2] '3.x'
      - name: Install dependencies
        run: |
            python -m pip install --upgrade pip
          pip install -r requirements.txt
      - name: Run tests
        run: |
          python -m unittest discover[3]
```

This workflow defines a CI pipeline that runs on every push or pull request to the `main` branch. It checks out the code, sets up Python, installs dependencies, and runs the tests.

3. Integrate with Version Control: Connect your CI/CD platform to your version control system (e.g., GitHub, GitLab, Bitbucket) to trigger builds and tests automatically on code changes.

4. Monitor and Analyze: Monitor the results of your CI builds and tests. Analyze test reports and code coverage to identify areas for improvement and ensure the quality of your automation.

Best Practices for CI with Automation

- **Start simple:** Begin with a basic CI workflow and gradually add more complex steps as needed.
- **Test frequently:** Run tests on every code commit to catch errors early.
- **Use a dedicated test environment:** Isolate your CI environment from production to avoid conflicts and ensure consistent test results.
- **Automate deployments:** Extend your CI pipeline to automate deployments to streamline the release process.

- **Monitor and analyze:** Track CI metrics and analyze test results to identify trends and improve your automation over time.

By implementing continuous integration for your automation projects, you can establish a robust development process that ensures the quality, reliability, and maintainability of your automation scripts. This leads to faster feedback loops, increased confidence, and more efficient automation workflows.

Chapter 11: Introduction to Machine Learning for Automation

Basic Machine Learning Concepts

Machine learning, a subfield of artificial intelligence, empowers computers to learn from data without explicit programming. By identifying patterns and relationships in data, machine learning algorithms can make predictions, automate decisions, and adapt to new information. This capability opens up exciting possibilities for enhancing automation, enabling more intelligent and dynamic workflows.

Core Components of Machine Learning

1. **Data:** The foundation of machine learning. Algorithms learn from data, identifying patterns and relationships to build models. Data can be structured (e.g., tables with rows and columns) or unstructured (e.g., text, images, audio).
2. **Tasks:** The specific problems that machine learning algorithms aim to solve. Common tasks include:
   - **Classification:** Assigning data points to predefined categories (e.g., spam detection, image recognition).

- **Regression:** Predicting a continuous value (e.g., stock price prediction, temperature forecasting).
- **Clustering:** Grouping similar data points together (e.g., customer segmentation, anomaly detection).
- **Dimensionality Reduction:** Reducing the number of features in a dataset while preserving important information.
- **Reinforcement Learning:** Training agents to make decisions in an environment to maximize rewards (e.g., game playing, robotics).

3. **Models:** Representations of the patterns and relationships learned from data. Models are used to make predictions or decisions on new data.

4. **Algorithms:** The methods used to learn from data and build models. Different algorithms are suited for different tasks and data types. Common algorithms include:
   - **Linear Regression:** Predicts a continuous value based on a linear relationship with input features.
   - **Logistic Regression:** Predicts the probability of a data point belonging to a specific category.

- **Decision Trees:** Creates a tree-like model to make decisions based on a series of rules.
- **Support Vector Machines (SVMs):** Finds the optimal hyperplane to separate data points into different categories.
- **Naive Bayes:** Applies Bayes' theorem to classify data based on the probability of features belonging to different classes.
- **k-Nearest Neighbors (k-NN):** Classifies data points based on the classes of their nearest neighbors.
- **k-Means Clustering:** Groups data points into clusters based on their similarity.

5. **Evaluation:** The process of assessing the performance of a machine learning model. Common evaluation metrics include:
   - **Accuracy:** The proportion of correctly classified instances.
   - **Precision:** The proportion of true positive predictions[1] among all positive predictions.
   - **Recall:** The proportion of true positive predictions among all actual[2] positive instances.

- **F1-score:** A harmonic mean of precision and recall.[3]
- **Mean Squared Error (MSE):** The average squared difference between predicted and actual values in regression.

Types of Machine Learning

- **Supervised Learning:** Algorithms learn from labeled data (data with known input-output pairs) to predict outcomes on new data. Examples include classification and regression.
- **Unsupervised Learning:** Algorithms learn from unlabeled data (data without known outputs) to discover patterns and structures. Examples include clustering and dimensionality reduction.
- **Reinforcement Learning:** Algorithms learn through trial and error, interacting with an environment and receiving feedback in the form of rewards or penalties.[4]

The Machine Learning Workflow

1. **Data Collection:** Gather the data needed for training your model.

2. **Data Preprocessing:** Clean, transform, and prepare the data for the learning algorithm.
3. **Feature Engineering:** Select, transform, or create relevant features that improve model performance.
4. **Model Selection:** Choose an appropriate algorithm based on the task and data.
5. **Training:** Train the model on the prepared data.
6. **Evaluation:** Assess the model's performance using appropriate metrics.
7. **Hyperparameter Tuning:** Adjust the model's parameters to optimize its performance.
8. **Deployment:** Deploy the trained model to make predictions on new data.

Machine Learning in Automation

Machine learning can enhance automation in various ways:

- **Intelligent Decision Making:** Use machine learning models to make more informed decisions in automation workflows.
- **Adaptive Automation:** Create automation systems that can adapt to changing conditions and learn from new data.

- **Predictive Automation:** Predict future events or behaviors to proactively trigger automation actions.
- **Pattern Recognition:** Identify patterns in data to automate tasks like anomaly detection or classification.

By understanding these basic machine learning concepts, you can begin to explore the potential of machine learning to enhance your automation solutions and create more intelligent and dynamic workflows.

Using `scikit-learn` for Automation

`scikit-learn` is a powerful and versatile Python library for machine learning. It provides a wide range of algorithms for classification, regression, clustering, dimensionality reduction,[1] model selection, and preprocessing. Its user-friendly API and comprehensive documentation make it a popular choice for both beginners and experienced machine learning practitioners. In the context of automation, `scikit-learn` can be a valuable tool for building intelligent and adaptive workflows.

Key Features of `scikit-learn`

1. **Variety of Algorithms:** `scikit-learn` offers a vast collection of algorithms for various machine learning tasks, including:
   - **Classification:** Logistic Regression, Support Vector Machines (SVMs), Decision Trees, Random Forests, Naive Bayes.
   - **Regression:** Linear Regression, Support Vector Regression (SVR), Decision Tree Regression, Random Forest Regression.
   - **Clustering:** k-Means, DBSCAN, Hierarchical Clustering.
   - **Dimensionality Reduction:** Principal Component Analysis (PCA), t-SNE.
2. **Simple and Consistent API:** `scikit-learn` follows a consistent API design, making it easy to learn and use different algorithms. The general workflow involves:
   - **Creating an estimator object:** Instantiate the desired algorithm.
   - **Fitting the model to data:** Train the model on your data using the `fit()` method.
   - **Making predictions:** Use the trained model to make predictions on new data using the `predict()` method.

3. **Data Preprocessing:** `scikit-learn` provides tools for data preprocessing, including:
    - **Scaling:** Standardizing or normalizing features to a specific range.
    - **Encoding categorical features:** Converting categorical variables into numerical representations.
    - **Imputation:** Handling missing values.
    - **Feature selection:** Selecting relevant features.
4. **Model Selection and Evaluation:** `scikit-learn` offers tools for:
    - **Splitting data:** Dividing data into training and testing sets.
    - **Cross-validation:** Evaluating model performance using different data splits.
    - **Hyperparameter tuning:** Optimizing model parameters using techniques like Grid Search or Randomized Search.
    - **Metrics:** Calculating various evaluation metrics like accuracy, precision, recall, F1-score, etc.
5. **Pipelines:** `scikit-learn`'s `Pipeline` class allows you to chain multiple steps together, creating a single, cohesive workflow for data

preprocessing, model training, and prediction.

Example (building a classification pipeline):

Python

```
from sklearn.pipeline import Pipeline
from sklearn.impute import SimpleImputer
from         sklearn.preprocessing[2]        import
StandardScaler
from         sklearn.linear_model         import
LogisticRegression[3]

# Create a pipeline
pipeline = Pipeline([
                                    ('imputer',
SimpleImputer(strategy='mean')),
   ('scaler', StandardScaler()),
   ('classifier', LogisticRegression())
])

# Fit the pipeline[4] to your data
pipeline.fit(X_train, y_train)

# Make predictions
predictions = pipeline.predict(X_test)[5]
```

This code defines a pipeline that imputes missing values, scales the features, and then trains a logistic regression model.

Automating Tasks with `scikit-learn`

- **Data Analysis and Preprocessing:** Automate data cleaning, transformation, and feature engineering tasks using `scikit-learn`'s preprocessing tools.
- **Model Training and Selection:** Automate the process of training and evaluating different machine learning models to find the best performing one for your task.
- **Predictive Modeling:** Integrate trained machine learning models into your automation workflows to make predictions and automate decisions.
- **Anomaly Detection:** Use unsupervised learning algorithms to automate the detection of anomalies or outliers in your data.
- **Dynamic Workflows:** Create automation workflows that adapt and learn from new data using online learning techniques.

Example (automating anomaly detection):

Python

```
from        sklearn.ensemble         import
IsolationForest

# Create an IsolationForest model
model = IsolationForest()

# Fit the model to your data
model.fit(X_train)

# Predict anomalies
anomaly_scores                              =
model.decision_function(X_test)
anomalies = X_test[anomaly_scores < -0.5]
# Adjust threshold as needed
```

This code trains an Isolation Forest model to detect anomalies in your data.

By leveraging the capabilities of `scikit-learn`, you can build more intelligent and adaptive automation solutions that learn from data and improve over time. This opens up new possibilities for automating complex tasks and creating more efficient and dynamic workflows.

Examples of ML-powered Automation

The integration of machine learning (ML) with automation is revolutionizing various industries and processes. By leveraging ML's ability to learn from data and make predictions, we can create automation solutions that are more intelligent, adaptive, and efficient. Here are some compelling examples of how ML is being used to power automation across different domains:

1. Customer Service and Support

- **Chatbots:** ML-powered chatbots can understand natural language and provide automated customer support, answering questions, resolving issues, and escalating complex queries to human agents.
- **Sentiment Analysis:** Analyze customer feedback from emails, surveys, or social media to automatically categorize sentiment (positive, negative, neutral) and prioritize responses.
- **Personalized Recommendations:** Recommend products or services to customers based on their past behavior and preferences.

2. Business Process Automation

- **Invoice Processing:** ML algorithms can extract information from invoices, automate data entry, and route invoices for approval, reducing manual effort and improving accuracy.
- **Fraud Detection:** Detect fraudulent transactions or activities by analyzing patterns and anomalies in data.
- **Risk Assessment:** Assess credit risk, insurance risk, or other types of risk using ML models.

3. IT Operations and Management

- **Predictive Maintenance:** Predict equipment failures or maintenance needs based on sensor data and historical trends, enabling proactive maintenance and reducing downtime.
- **Network Security:** Detect and prevent cyberattacks by analyzing network traffic and identifying malicious patterns.
- **Resource Optimization:** Optimize resource allocation in cloud environments based on usage patterns and predicted demand.

4. Marketing and Sales

- **Lead Scoring:** Rank leads based on their likelihood to convert into customers, allowing sales teams to prioritize their efforts.
- **Targeted Advertising:** Deliver personalized ads to users based on their interests and demographics.
- **Content Recommendation:** Recommend relevant content to users based on their browsing history and preferences.

5. Healthcare

- **Medical Diagnosis:** Assist in diagnosing diseases by analyzing medical images, patient records, and other data.
- **Personalized Treatment:** Recommend personalized treatment plans based on patient characteristics and disease progression.
- **Drug Discovery:** Accelerate drug discovery by analyzing molecular structures and predicting their properties.

6. Manufacturing and Supply Chain

- **Quality Control:** Automate quality inspection by analyzing images or sensor data to identify defects.

- **Demand Forecasting:** Predict future demand for products to optimize inventory management and production planning.
- **Supply Chain Optimization:** Optimize logistics and transportation routes using ML algorithms.

7. Human Resources

- **Resume Screening:** Automate resume screening by analyzing candidate profiles and matching them to job requirements.
- **Candidate Assessment:** Assess candidate skills and suitability using ML-powered assessments.
- **Employee Churn Prediction:** Predict employee attrition and identify factors contributing to turnover.

8. Finance

- **Algorithmic Trading:** Use ML algorithms to make automated trading decisions based on market data and trends.
- **Portfolio Optimization:** Optimize investment portfolios based on risk tolerance and financial goals.
- **Fraud Prevention:** Detect and prevent financial fraud by analyzing transaction patterns and identifying anomalies.

These examples demonstrate the transformative potential of ML-powered automation across diverse industries. By combining ML's ability to learn from data with automation's ability to execute tasks, we can create solutions that are more intelligent, efficient, and adaptive, leading to improved productivity, better decision-making, and enhanced outcomes.

CONCLUSION

As you reach the end of this journey through the world of Python automation, you've gained a powerful set of tools and techniques to transform the way you work and interact with technology. From automating mundane tasks to building intelligent systems, Python's versatility and extensive ecosystem have empowered you to tackle a wide range of automation challenges.

Throughout this book, we've explored the essential concepts and practical applications of Python automation. You've learned how to:

- **Master the fundamentals of Python:** You've built a solid foundation in Python programming, understanding data types, control flow, functions, and object-oriented programming.
- **Interact with the operating system:** You can now manage files and directories, execute commands, schedule tasks, and work with environment variables.
- **Automate web tasks:** You've acquired the skills to scrape data from websites, interact with APIs, and control web browsers.

- **Enhance communication:** You can send and receive emails programmatically and integrate with messaging platforms like Slack.
- **Control graphical applications:** You've delved into GUI automation, enabling you to automate interactions with desktop applications.
- **Harness the power of databases:** You can connect to databases, extract and manipulate data, and generate reports.
- **Build robust and reliable automation:** You've learned how to implement error handling, debugging techniques, and testing strategies to ensure your automation solutions are resilient and maintainable.
- **Unlock the potential of machine learning:** You've been introduced to basic machine learning concepts and how to apply them to create intelligent automation solutions.

The Future of Automation

The field of automation is constantly evolving, with new technologies and trends emerging rapidly. As you continue your automation journey, keep these key trends in mind:

- **Artificial Intelligence (AI) and Machine Learning (ML):** AI and ML will play an increasingly important role in automation, enabling more intelligent and adaptive systems.
- **Robotic Process Automation (RPA):** RPA is gaining traction, allowing businesses to automate complex workflows that involve interactions with multiple applications.
- **Hyperautomation:** Hyperautomation aims to automate as many processes as possible, combining RPA with AI and ML to create end-to-end automation solutions.
- **Cloud Automation:** Cloud computing provides a scalable and flexible platform for automation, enabling you to deploy and manage automation solutions in the cloud.
- **The Internet of Things (IoT):** The IoT is generating vast amounts of data that can be used to automate processes and create smart environments.

Continuing Your Learning

Automation is a continuous learning process. To stay ahead of the curve and further develop your automation skills, consider:

- **Exploring advanced Python libraries and frameworks:** Delve deeper into libraries like `Selenium`, `Scrapy`, `pandas`, and `scikit-learn` to expand your automation capabilities.
- **Learning about cloud automation platforms:** Familiarize yourself with cloud platforms like AWS, Azure, and GCP and their automation services.
- **Staying updated on AI and ML advancements:** Keep abreast of the latest developments in AI and ML and how they can be applied to automation.
- **Joining online communities and forums:** Connect with other automation enthusiasts and professionals to share knowledge and learn from their experiences.
- **Building real-world automation projects:** Apply your skills to automate tasks in your own work or personal life to gain practical experience.

Embrace the Automation Mindset

As you continue to explore the world of automation, remember that it's not just about automating tasks; it's about embracing an automation mindset. This involves:

- **Identifying opportunities for automation:** Look for repetitive, time-consuming tasks that can be automated.
- **Breaking down complex processes:** Decompose complex workflows into smaller, automatable steps.
- **Thinking creatively about solutions:** Explore different approaches and tools to find the best automation solution for your needs.
- **Continuously improving and optimizing:** Refine your automation solutions over time to enhance their efficiency and effectiveness.

By embracing this mindset and continuing to develop your skills, you can unlock the full potential of automation and transform the way you work and interact with technology.

Congratulations on completing this journey into the world of Python automation! We hope this book has empowered you with the knowledge and tools to embark on a path of increased productivity, efficiency, and innovation.

www.ingramcontent.com/pod-product-compliance
Lightning Source LLC
LaVergne TN
LVHW052058060326
832903LV00061B/3398